The creativity of listening

The creativity of listening

Being there, reaching out

BILL KIRKPATRICK

DARTON·LONGMAN + TODD

I dedicate this book to my mother, Florence Kirkpatrick, Matron of the Kirkpatrick Nursing Home for the Elderly near Vancouver, BC, Canada, who nurtured me into a caring ministry, and all others who have shared so much of themselves with me.

First published in 2005 by
Darton, Longman and Todd Ltd
1 Spencer Court
140–142 Wandsworth High Street
London
SW18 4JJ

ISBN 0 232 52579 X

A catalogue record for this book is available from the British Library.

Designed by Sandie Boccacci
Phototypeset by Intype Libra Ltd
Printed and bound in Great Britain by
Page Bros, Norwich, Norfolk

Contents

Foreword

This book is the story of a love affair with God. Along the way we are privileged to be given access to some of the most intimate moments of a relationship where the listening ear of the lover dares to hear the whispers of his own heart, the voices of his dearest friends, the sufferings of countless individuals and the silent wisdom of the created order. Bill Kirkpatrick, even before he knew it consciously, has been in love with God throughout his life and in this veritable treasure house of a book he tells us something of the agony and the ecstasy of that relationship and of the mysteries revealed in the midst of a life's spiritual pilgrimage.

The outward events of Father Bill's life are remarkable enough. Born in Canada and trained as a nurse before he became a priest, he has somehow incorporated the whole world into his ministry of presence and what he calls 'co-creative listening' which, for many decades now, has been anchored in his beloved Earls Court in London. In the 1980s and 90s his fame as a pastor to the alienated and desperate – especially the young – was such that he was invited by the World Council of Churches to be a consultant to their HIV/AIDS unit. He travelled the globe in this capacity and we hear of visits to the Caribbean, India, Thailand, South Africa, Brazil and Australia. There are earlier accounts, too, of significant experiences at Taizé in France, at Assisi in Italy and in Sardinia where the vision of a beautiful woman sent him on his return home to consult both a psychiatrist and a priest. These journeys around the world are but a pale reflection, how-ever, of the inner journey which Father Bill seeks to describe with disarming openness and without a trace of self-inflation.

He lets us into the sanctuary of his intimate communion with a God who does not know how to reject but who, on the con-trary, offers total acceptance and infinite compassion. Safe in this relationship he is able to celebrate his own being as a gay man and to enter without fear into the suffering of the sick, the mentally afflicted and the dying. What is more he affirms his priesthood with confidence and points to a future where the Church will abandon its censorious attitudes and begin at last to love as Christ loves. The pastor becomes the prophet and the outcome is a book which is not only deeply moving but will also serve to strengthen and inspire all those who are brought to the verge of despair by the current divisions and acrimony both between Christians and between the great World Faiths.

This sense of hope beyond despair is further nourished by the remarkable cloud of witnesses which Father Bill calls to testify in these pages. He offers us the choicest fruits of a library of spiritual and secular writers and displays an unerring ability to find the exact quotation to illustrate a theme or to reinforce a point of view. To read this book is therefore also to be challenged to pursue a whole course of study for which Father Bill has indirectly provided an extensive list of recommended texts. The pastor and prophet is also an unselfconscious scholar to whom future students will be much indebted.

Pastor, priest, prophet, scholar and, finally, poet. Not only does Father Bill include prayers and reflections which he has himself couched in poetic form but there is also a lyrical quality about the text as a whole. Perhaps this is a further indication of the 'practical mysticism' which permeates the book and of which the 'creativity of listening' is the primary and most potent example. For Father Bill, our ability to listen in depth to each other is the key to those personal encounters which allow God to enter our lives. Listening for him is a sacred art and, like poetry, it gives access to a world both within and beyond the experiences of our daily existence. And yet it demands a willingness to be fully present to the other and involves the inevitable risk of confronting ourselves and discovering the full extent of our own woundedness. This is a book, then, which is likely to disturb as well as delight if we really dare to listen.

Brian Thorne
Emeritus Professor of Counselling
University of East Anglia, Norwich

Acknowledgements

I have always believed, indeed I know for a fact, that we do nothing on our own. There are always others with their differing ways and viewpoints to assist us in our endeavours. This, I believe, is because we are all born to be co-creators rather than co-destructors. Equally, there is always present the 'mysterious other', which has many names or no name. For me all caring is trinitarian.

There are many people I would especially like to acknowledge in the making of this book. John Todd, co-founder of Darton, Longman & Todd, in 1989 said to me, 'Bill, you have been in Earls Court now for ten years, there must be a book there. I would like you to write it.' Fifteen years later, his request has been fulfilled. I wish to acknowledge the support and helpful criticisms of Jim Hall and Richie McMullen, which only partners feel they can offer. I am fully aware that I alone am responsible for this book, but no one creates on their own. Any book must be the result of a co-creative venture. Therefore I am thankful to many people upfront and behind the scenes for the help they have offered by their differing expertise. I have been, and I am, blessed by them all.

I am grateful to the following people who have read the manuscript through its different stages of gestation; it is much richer for their time, their comments, their healthy criticisms and their continuing support: James Cairn-Cross, Jim Hall, Sister Eva Heymann, Revd Canon Eric James, Brian Jones, Peter Johnson, John Laing, Anthony and Robina Masters, Richie McMullen, Frank Nugent, Dr Helen Oppenheimer, James Roose-Evans, Dr Alan Sippert, Fiona Sketch, Dr Heather Snidle, Dr Bryan Teixeira, Dr Verena Tschudin.

We are all fully aware that secretaries are worth more than their weight in gold as they battle with our scribbles and the constant changes we make to our manuscripts. For this book I am indebted to Betty Goodrum for her work on the first major draft, and to Mary Warner for her efforts on the final one.

Most authors need quiet, embracing spaces to help their work along. This vital need has been provided for me at various times and places by Maurice and Hilda Laing at the home 'Reculver'; by their son John at Great Coldharbour Farm; and by Ursula Vertone and Bob Hull in West Vancouver, Canada.

What would any author do without the expertise and guiding hand of our editors? Thanks is a small word that contains so much – to Brendan Walsh who recognized the book's potential; to Virginia Hearn, my encouraging editor, who has helped me enormously in 'polishing up the jewel within a rough stone'; and to all the editorial team at Darton, Longman & Todd.

21 October 2004

Introduction

The title of this book arises from my awareness of the important role played by listening in the healing of those who need to be heard. Thousands of books, millions of words, have been written on how we might learn to listen, in order to hear and respond. Countless people throughout my life, both those who are living and many who have died, have contributed by giving me the privilege of learning how to listen, hear and respond. I have learned from my own experience of being heard by various listeners, who have affirmed me and thus made me feel that I mattered as a person.

Why have I written this book? Its impetus is my increasing awareness of what I call 'the rise of non-listening' among individuals and society. We are losing the ability to listen in-depth to each other. As a result there is increasing depersonalisation, and a corresponding number of individuals feel themselves disenfranchised. This can and does lead to violence, towards oneself and others. In contrast, meaningful dialogue is nurtured through the *sacred art* of listening. Being heard empowers us to gain a greater sense of worth and affirms our innate dignity. The essential message of *The Creativity of Listening* is that I believe it is crucial that we make time to hear one another in such a way that we will be able to hear whatever is taking place within ourselves. I believe that global listening is, and must be, centred in the personal meeting of one with the other; and, in the widest sense, in the family (whatever the family is today) – in local, national and international communities, all nurtured by the dignity of respect, truth and justice.

I write for the many people who are involved in the differing activities of personal and shared caring; and specifically for those whose prime work is to be involved as listeners, either on a professional or a volunteer level. This book echoes my indebtedness to many people in my early life as a nursing assistant in the Kirkpatrick Nursing Home, where I first became involved in the profession of caring. Since then I have been encouraged and trained for the sacred ministry of hearing through listening by many people – wounded, rejected seekers and others – who one way or another have come into my orbit of concern. They have shown me that effective caring may flow between people who are possessed or dominated by nothing save love's hope, the kind that nurtures the compassion of empathy. They have constantly reminded me that we are called and directed, from deep within ourselves, to be co-listeners, co-healers, co-seekers and co-speakers.

Being there

When I am asked 'What do you do?' I reply that I am around for anyone, with a 'pair of big ears'. I hope simply to 'be there', as one who is committed to hearing through listening. I have spent most of my life 'being there', reaching out towards outcasts, the wounded and others. Being there is being alongside another person in whatever way he or she desires me to be, thereby affirming that that person matters not only to me as a carer, but to him or herself. Being there, in this area of need, has given me a deeper awareness of my own need to be heard, that my inner-most self is both vulnerable and valuable. However, I am still faced with the ultimate questions about life and death. What do these questions mean for me as a Christian, as a man, as a priest – who happens to be gay – and, far more importantly, as a member of the community Bishop Tutu called the 'rainbow people of God'?

Being there has taught me, and still teaches me, much about being a 'spiritual' – rather than a 'religious' – person. Being there continues to inform me a great deal about the gifts of differing lifestyles and situations, about being vulnerable with the honesty of truth. Being there continues to teach me about the pain of loving and of being loved – the pain of pre-bereavement; about waiting, about dying and grief – the pain of post-bereavement. Being there is gradually revealing to me the mysteries of the love of God as creator and ultimate lover. These mysteries nurture my understanding, and my acceptance, that to love and be loved is every person's natural birthright, even though millions throughout the world continue to be deprived of such loving.

Being there affirms for me that there is no them or us. We are all vulnerable to our frailties, to disease and death. These too are our natural birthright. Being there informs me about receiving care from those who have allowed me, and who continue to allow me, into their sacred space and areas of special need. Being there has shown me how vital it is to drop labels that separate and diminish dignity, as I reach out from within a co-caring, mutually liberating commitment.

In my work I am constantly required to ask questions of myself, to reflect on my gifts and limitations, my areas of vulnerability and my imperfections. In order to be there for others, I have to be aware of my own needs, to ensure that I have come to terms with events in my life, with my sexuality, with my personal losses and bereavements. I need to ask myself, am I willing to be there with the truth of my frailties, my strengths, as a humanised presence of God, of the kind that does not know how to reject?

These questions and many more help me to keep in touch with myself and those who invite me into their sacred spaces. I believe it is my responsibility, my vocation if you like, simply to be there without counting the cost. Indeed it is not easy, as I attempt to offer and receive the gifts of mutual care in recognition of the fact that we are all living, dying, and living once more, as we flow with our differing gifts into the greater mystery labelled death.

Being there as a listener who attempts to hear is not always easy. As a priest and minister, I have a concern for all who come to me, as a channel of the healing energies and boundless love of the Holy Spirit.

Co-creation

When I use the prefix 'co' before words like 'creative' and 'healing', I am attempting to share with you what is a truth for me, that is, that I have done nothing of my own – even though at times it may appear that I have. I could not have developed as a person without someone who needed me to listen unconditionally; the reflective act of hearing through listening fulfils my own need to be authenticated as a person of value, not only by others but also by myself. This confirms for me a basic necessity, that for our lives to be full, we must accept the fact that we are born not only to be with God but also with each other. We are so wonderfully created that we have the choice of being either co-creative or co-destructive with each other. We are co-creative whenever we are being the truth of ourselves and allowing this truth to authenticate each other; whenever we are in a relation-ship of love that is growth-enabling; whenever we express our faith in others as well as in ourselves.

What is co-creation? It is letting go and allowing the mystery of God to create through us and with us that which God has the need to create. It is said that we were created to be God's hand-men and hand-women, to assist in the work of fulfilling his desire for all to share in God's handiwork. We are born, I believe, to realise our fullest potential through each other, and for me this is, or should be, an ongoing co-creative event. It will not be so if I live off others in a negative way, having my needs fulfilled at the expense of other people. My growth continues through being there for other people who seek my concern and atten-tiveness. In this activity, I am growing through our mutual need to be needed – the source of our co-creative, co-healing poten-tial. Being involved in the ministry of healing for most of my life has informed me of its potential to achieve co-healing, between the person labelled patient (or whatever) and the person labelled healer (or whatever).

I suspect that, like myself, many involved in the ministry of care are doing so because of their own healing needs. Provided that these needs are not greater than those of the person we are caring for (or with), then the channel of the healing grace of God is released in a way that is beneficial for all involved. We learn to care through having been cared for, and it is through caring that we learn how to be co-caring of each other.

So I speak of being 'co-creative' whenever we are affirming each other into a life worth living and dying for; whenever we are being the truth of ourselves towards each other; whenever we empower growth; whenever we express that each of us matters. With this potential for co-creation, we are making a powerful affirmation of each other's worth, one which is two-sided: it enables me to continue to grow and evolve into the 'sacred work' of hearing through listening. Whenever I am entrusted to 'be there', offering my full attention and response as a listener, I believe that I and the person to whom I am listening are co-creatively linked.

Seeking and receiving

I have spent many hours in dialogue with myself and others about the following conundrum – do we hear in order to listen, or do we listen in order to hear, or is it both? We can describe the person being listened to and heard, i.e. the speaker, as the seeker. Yet I believe that in fact both speaker and listener are seekers. The listener seeks to hear where the speaker is coming from, while the speaker trusts that the listener is hearing. Therefore the listener and the speaker are co-seekers. The speaker is searching for a way and an understanding through the presenting problem or situation. The listener, through hearing, is seeking a way of assisting the speaker to become self-empowering.

There is no doubt that both listener and speaker are offering as well as receiving. When this is recognised, we are able to release together the healing energies latent within ourselves. As listener and speaker we both offer and receive care. I try to offer all of myself, through my presence and the attentiveness of my hearing through listening, to the all-ness of the speaker. A similar activity flows from the speaker towards myself.

I am 'being there' from within the still point of my soul, without any preconceived ideas or expectations of what may or may not occur between the seeker and myself. I am there for all those who are searching for the mystery of their meaning and purpose in life.

I believe in the use of inclusive language. I believe all are of equal value in the eyes, the heart-soul of God. 'Male and Female he created them all' (Gen. 1:27). In recognition of this fact, whenever possible I will alternate the usage of these gender terms. I believe it is crucial that we recognise each other as equals with differing, unique gifts and experiences. I do so knowing that both seeker and listener are involved in the work of listening, hearing and responding. There is little doubt in my mind that this work is the most co-creative and co-healing adventure we share.

I am eternally indebted to many people, of all ages, throughout my life who have listened to me and heard me in such a manner that I have been released to become the person I am daily becoming; to those who have recognised the 'hidden me' and my potential for growth. I am equally indebted to all who have had the courage to share the uniqueness of their pains with me. Listening is the key to releasing our innate power, and to healing all our wounds visible and invisible, personal and corporate.

Part I

Listening and hearing

Compassionate listening is a key to transforming the world.

Jack Kornfield, After the Ecstasy, the Laundry, *2001*

1

Listening to hear

We can heal ourselves
if we learn to listen
with our ears
with our eyes
with our minds
with our feelings
with our love.
It is important
that we listen
to God's love in our heart
to God's voice in our conscience.
It is healing to listen
to our self-value
to our bodies
to our habits
to our potential.
What therapy we may find
in the symphony of nature,
in the music that surrounds us,
in the humour of living.
We are called to listen
in silence
in prayer
at work
in the noise

BK

What is listening? It is the ability to hear sounds, voices, and vibrations emanating from oneself and others, through the offering of focused, willed attention. It is the key that 'opens the way' towards other people. It is an invaluable asset. Clearly it is an art; with continual practice it can become a great art, but for most people today it is a lost art. Although listening is instinctive, we need to learn constantly how to do it, how to be it. That is why it is so difficult. We need to learn how to listen again and again, and to listen to new things, new words and new sounds. If we desire to go forward in life we can do it only one step at a time. Each step has its distinctive 'word' that needs to be discerned.

David Brandon makes a very important point when he writes, 'Listeners do need a beginner's mind, that strips away our fixed notions and dogmas. You can't go in with preconceived ideas of how to "fix-up" the situation. You have to ask people who need, and empower them to "find their own solutions" ' (Brandon, p. 141). In saying this he echoes my own feeling that, at some deep level, soul level if you like, we have the answers. We go to a listener for assistance, in order to help us recognise that we have our own answer waiting to come into the light of our consciousness, thereby releasing energy for ongoing growth.

Brandon highlights the key question, 'Why bother with listening?' His answer is that at a fundamental level, no relationship can exist without some form of communication, because of its reciprocal nature, that forms the very fabric of any relationship' (Brandon, pp. 111–12).

Kinds of listening

Listening is generally understood to mean being attentive to some audible stimulus, whether it is the voice, music, or some other sound. At this point, however, since no other convenient term exists, we must extend its meaning. Although speech is the main form of communication, it is by no means the only one. We continually transmit information about ourselves using many channels apart from the actual spoken word. Our tone of voice, accent, speech patterns and choice of words tell a great deal more about ourselves and our thinking. Alongside these means we make use, consciously or otherwise, of facial expressions, bodily movements, posture and even dress. If we are to understand fully what another person is trying to tell us, then we have no alternative but to be attentive to all these channels of communication. We must listen to the whole person, not merely to his words.

The term 'listen' has three apparent meanings: the first is to hear; the second is like the meaning of the French *connaître*, to 'understand'; and the third is a command to pay attention. In the religious life obedience is listening.

However, it is crucial that we as listeners remember there is another kind of listening, one which can be of immense value. It is 'listening with understanding', about which Carl Rogers has much to say. This is the attempt to see the other person's ideas and attitudes from her point of view, to sense how it feels for her. It implies understanding *with*, rather than *of*, the person concerned. There is no doubt in my mind that the action of hearing through listening is crucial in itself. The truth is that ultimately it is the personality of the listener that is the key factor in establishing a positive relationship with the seeker, so essential if the seeker's innate healing energies are to flow.

Listening is a multidimensional activity that is complex, demanding and mutually enriching. Through listening we are privileged to hear what the seeker is saying and to discover who she is as a unique person. It is also about hospitality offered by the listener that I might offer hospitality to myself. I would say that hearing through listening is a form of spirituality, and being heard is vitally important for our growth.

Listening is touch, one of the most ancient forms of healing and comfort. The listener is someone who is in touch with herself and so is able to be in touch with others, in such a way that the other person is also able to be there for herself. The touch to which I refer is not solely a physical experience of tactile communication. It is much more a recognition and honouring of the fullness of the other person. The listener who, for whatever reason, is unable to touch others will never come to know them as people. The listener who is unafraid to touch, to embrace, is a person who is unafraid of being human, who has put shame and fear in their proper perspective. The fact is that there must be a touching of the right kind, offered with respect for the other person, if listening is to take place.

Joan Searle points out that hearing through listening is not just the prerogative of the professionals. We all have the capability, although it requires training to fully develop the skill:

certainly it does not come naturally. This is why we must be aware of our limitations, and of equal importance to accept the fact we are in the presence of the seeker as an equal who is searching for an answer, or at least an explanation or an insight that may be of some assistance in the meaning of a decision. It is important we are aware of being invited as a guest into each other's sacred space of being, for sharing whatever with a sensitivity of attentive concern for the seeker. This is why as listeners it is essential we are acutely aware of the differing skills that are required.

(Searle, *The Importance of Listening*, p. 4)

Hearing through listening is liberating in that it releases the flow of communication between the seeker and the listener through its quality of mutual trust. Respect is recognising and giving value to the seeker. It is affirming him or her as someone who matters, who is unique, worthwhile and created through the Creator's desiring, whether this is recognised or accepted or not. This freely expressed attitude says to the seeker, 'You are free to risk becoming your own person'. As two people caught up in the miracle of love's true endeavouring, not only does the seeker matter, so does the listener. This activity of mutual mattering reminds me that I have the capacity and will to be the listener. I lay aside my own thoughts and 'let go', so that I am listening to the seeker with the depth of my openness. It is from within the friendship of concern that I attune myself to the mystery of the other person, as we stand together within the holy ground of each other's uniqueness.

Listening to the Soul
Ram Dass asks, 'what is it then, this power of the voice to reach down deep and turn us around? It is the *power of being*. The voice is *the muscle of soul*. It can embody and express the heights and depths of human experience' (Dass, *How Can I Help?*, p. 169, italics mine).

It has been said that 'the body is the ear; similarly the ear is the body'. Can it not also be said that 'the soul is the ear and the ear is the soul'? Listening to each other is *centring in*. As listeners we are given the privilege of being allowed into the deeper sacredness of the soul; into the inner pain unique to the person sharing themselves with us. However, we shall not be allowed into this centre unless we have listened carefully to the superficial, to the bearable level the speaker is able to cope with in any particular period. In fact it may require many sessions together, or even many months, before the person feels strong and safe enough for signs of a breakthrough to emerge. During this time of waiting we must hold the speaker within the embrace of our patient listening. There is simply no point in being in the activity of listening unless we are *prepared to be patient* with the other person's mystery. We are there with the seeker's permission, through agreeing to 'be there'. The seeker, like everyone else, including oneself, has a unique story which they long to share with someone, to have it heard and understood in such a way that they themselves may hear and understand its meaning. Handled badly, through one's own excitement at the achievement of a breakthrough, the revealing moment may frighten the speaker back into the depths of fear, of confusion. To listen sensitively to the seeker's agony may often stir up one's own agony. If the listener has not dealt with this, a reversal of roles may very well develop which may be quite damaging to the seeker's expectation of the listener's ability to be fully with him.

Carl Jung listened to so much darkness, as he called it, and he felt the pain of others so deeply, that he found it absolutely necessary to go away one month in four in order to discharge the pain he had picked up through listening. A similar break is crucial for all of us who are attempting to listen to the varying shades of darkness, the mysteriousness of the speaker. We are seldom given the sacred privilege of seeing others in the truth of their nakedness.

It is through this kind of listening that we are struck by the mystery of the human soul, the utter humanity of each carrying such a mystery within. None of us is ever ushered into the deepest recesses of another soul unless our lives and our actions express some of this awe. Something instinctive in the seeker keeps this sacred centre closed to many, except for those who have developed this kind of reverence and are able to listen with a sense of awe.

Through hearing we are in communion, because we are communicating, and thus affirming that the seeker matters to us.

We come to appreciate the courage of the seeker who dares to reveal their innermost feelings to us. In so doing we experience the seeker as being a 'goodness bearer' of mutual healing. Such listening in depth is a prayerful activity, a kind of spiritual experience of being an enabler. We authenticate others through our own courageous openness to receiving the new insights, new knowledge and new awareness that are revealed to us through the seeker. The identity of the caring person as listener is born out of the intangible and creative tension between self-affirmation and self-denial; between self-realisation and self-sacrifice; between self-authentication and self-denying. These are all co-creative opposites, causing us to be aware that we cannot offer what we do not already have, or that we are afraid of acknowledging what we have to offer. 'Self-sacrifice is an act of total responsibility whereby we take complete hold of ourselves and place ourselves at the disposition of the whole; we cease to be apart and become one with the whole. We then "re-present" the whole' (Nichol, *Holiness*, p. 19).

Four ears of hearing
When we perform the activity of hearing through listening, of listening in depth, we are made aware of the fact that we have four ears of hearing. The first ear enables me to hear myself; the second to hear the other person; the third to hear the meaning of silence in differing situations; and the fourth to hear the group or community. We hear ourselves through the mechanics of the outer and inner ears, using the latter to hear through listening to that which speaks to us from deep within the heart-soul of our lives.

It is important that the listener develops a state of consciousness where she is genuinely open to hearing through listening on all levels. Freud called it 'free-floating attention', Reich called it 'listening with the third ear', Carl Rogers called it 'intuitive sensing'. It is what Krishnamurti calls 'choiceless awareness'; it is in fact 'whole person awareness', as we listen with our first, second, third and fourth ears. With whatever ear we are listening we suspend thinking in order to 'be there' with the seeker, offering the empathy of non-possessive warmth. Such warmth reveals the depth of our listening and of ourselves as real persons genuinely concerned for the seeker, as we share in the listening circle of love's healing endeavours.

The listener should be aware and able to accept the fact that she listens within a restricted range of sympathies and abilities, but that through endeavouring to hear and be aware the listener as well as the seeker is travelling on her respective journey through the uniqueness of her differing wounds of life. Surface listening is easy and requires no more than that we keep our ears open, while listening in depth is an active process involving commitment, through which we offer the respect of love as a way of affirming and encouraging the seeker towards a greater sense of liberation, acceptance and worth. The listener who desires to experience this kind of listening must be ready to listen with their whole being. Depth listening makes the speaker real, as one who matters; it allows him 'to be', to feel less fearful and more hopeful of flowing towards a fullness of 'being', of experiencing the raison d'être of his life with its moods, pains and joys.

The Enabling Embrace of the Still Centre

Listening can be very disturbing at times. The question then is, what can I as a listener do? Initially I should be realistic about how much I am able to cope with. Some days this will be easier than others. Ordinarily I can cope with a moderate amount of verbal abuse, and can recognise that the source of such behaviour may very well be linked with painful or even frightening memories for the seeker, with unresolved sorrows, anger or anxieties. There is much that can be done by accepting calmly what the seeker is attempting to reveal at these times. As the listener, I can accept a hostile verbal attack if I am able to understand the source of the hostility. If the seeker can be seen as someone who desires to be accepted, loved, but who at that moment must pretend the opposite, it is possible to react in a positive manner. A calm acceptance of the seeker's fury is often followed by an apology at a later date. I must abandon myself to the experiences of the seeker without letting go of who I am. George's story, like many others, reminds me that if I can be a 'still centre' within the hurricane of different situations, changes will occur for both seeker and listener.

George arrived at my door one day wanting to be baptised. When he had received the sacrament of baptism, he collapsed on to the floor. Soon afterwards he started seeing me on a monthly basis. These meetings always started and ended in a similar fashion; I rapidly learned how difficult it was to be with someone who constantly abused me, verbally and occasionally physically. Through these encounters, I learned that I could stay with George only to the extent that I was able to maintain a 'still centre' within myself.

Gradually he became less abusive, so that I could begin to find a sense of where his behaviour might be coming from. Slowly he found the ability to put into words a history of rejection, which he had experienced since he was born. Never having been accepted himself, he did not know how to accept others. It was revealed that he had been unwanted from the moment of conception, and remembered being told so by both his parents. Although now a man in his forties, he continued to feel this pain. I asked myself, was his conception due to lust rather than love? Certainly his anger suggested the former. George, I suggest, was born feeling the pain of not having been wanted even while in his mother's womb. His pain would only heal in time, through a sensitive embracing of love's healing energies, thereby enabling him to re-channel that pain from its negative to its co-creative potential.

A great deal of his pain was related to his constant demand for a sex change that was persistently being refused. Often during my meetings with George he would say, 'I know you are my counsellor, but I want to marry you. I know you are queer, you could be my husband.' Quite often he would become quite angry because I would not accept his proposal. He would say, 'Nobody wants me'; he would shout, 'And you are bloody well supposed to care. You're just as bad as all the rest of them!' For George this was yet another rejection in a lifetime of rejections. He had great difficulty in accepting that he was acceptable.

Some months after our meetings had ended he arrived one day quite out of the blue. Could I help him get a new flat from the local council? This I was able to do, and he did eventually move into a very comfortable flat. From then on I only heard from him via long telephone calls, always made from a box; either when he was in need or, on a few occasions, when he was in hospital. One evening, after not hearing from him for nearly five years, he rang me from his hospital bed. He had fallen on the snow in the street and had been taken to a hospital in the East End of London. Would I go to the chemist and get him shaving materials? Travelling from Earls Court in West London, I did so. When I arrived he was creating a fuss with the nurses. They had put him in a male ward and he wanted to be in a female ward. After much discussion with the nursing staff, they agreed he could have a single room off the female ward, whereupon he became a model patient.

Another time, during one of our sessions, I remember him telling me, 'I'm having a birthday next month, not that anyone bloody cares.' Our next appointment happened to be on his birthday, so I thought beforehand that I would make him a simple birthday cake. When I offered it to him, he threw it on to the floor, gave me a tirade of verbal abuse and stormed out. I suspect he still could not accept that he was being accepted for who he was, as a person in his own right.

Two or three years later I again heard from George. He was in a small psychiatric unit, having been found acting strangely on the street. The police had been called and he was admitted to the unit. Having been there a week he contacted me to get him out of 'this nutter's place'. He was to have an assessment about his possible discharge and they wanted a reference from me to assist in their deliberations. I explained I had known George for about 15 years, that he was quite an eccentric and could become verbally aggressive if he felt people were making fun of him. George was released. He rang and thanked me.

I did not hear from him again for five or more years, when he called to say, 'I'm OK, I won't be seeing you any more. Thanks for being a bloody good man, take care.'

Silence

Another key requirement of listening is the ability to maintain one's own silence without being troubled by the silence of the listener seeker. This mutuality of silence, while causing some tension, may be a way of liberation for the seeker. It is important not to become embarrassed or anxious about filling in the gaps of silence that will occur. The listener's role is to seek to understand the meaning of that silence. The silence may indicate a breakdown in communication as the speaker senses a change in the listener's attitude, possibly caused by uncertainty as to what the listener is expecting him to say. Equally it could mean that the seeker is contemplating more self-revelation and may be wondering how this will be interpreted by the listener.

Our listening demands a stillness of the contemplative mind – one must spend less time on one's own thoughts and worries. There is little doubt that silence at its best can draw the seeker out, while at the same time assuring him or her of the listener's attentiveness. Silence can act as a sounding board as it intensifies the effects of the spoken word. Ivan Mann writes: 'When we can live with our own silence, we can dare to be silent with others, offering not the silence of rejection but unobtrusive silence; "communicative silence", or words from the heart of love, spoken carefully, gently, though sometimes challengingly into the silence' (Mann, *A Double Thirst*, pp. 145–6).

As a listener, I must have the patience to wait on the seeker's words, taking time to digest inwardly the true meaning of words before assuming they have the same meaning as I would attribute to them. This means at best that I have the ability to offer my fullest attention in order to decipher what the words may mean to the seeker. It is important for the seeker to be aware of the fact that the word is *not* the meaning, just as the wrapping on the parcel is not the goods in the parcel. The word is not the object it names, just as a photo is not the person; the word is not the actual experience as expressed, just as the seeker's story is only a small part of this moment or period in her personal life journey.

The meanings I give to words are based on inferences and intuitions, not on facts. This means I may only be able to grasp an inkling of what the seeker means by the words and signals offered. At best, the listener can only guess their possible meanings. This is why it is crucial to have the courage of unknowing, to reflect on what has been heard and to confirm it with the speaker.

It is vitally important for the listener to be aware that meanings are not transmitted by oral communication alone. There are wordless sounds, pauses, silences, posture, stance, rapid or slow speech, as well as the seeker's general appearance including the colour or style of their clothing. Meanings emanate from the total person, not from words alone. 'Words don't mean, people mean', as Lewis Carroll observes in the dialogue between Humpty Dumpty and Alice.

It is through the 'Trinity' of unobtrusive observation, listening with intent, and reflection that I am better able to communicate with the seeker, and the seeker with myself. At best I will then begin to hear something of the inner meaning of confused words, the mixed symbols and erratic behaviour that may have no meaning for me and yet will have real meaning for the seeker. There is always so much more to learn through hearing by the listener and seeker within their mutual journey towards healing.

Aids to Effective Listening

The following are practical suggestions designed to help anyone engaged in the role of listener to one who seeks.

It is helpful to adopt a meditative approach towards being with the seeker in order to free oneself to being fully attentive. In preparing for each encounter, it is important to pay attention to the physical environment, and to provide an atmosphere that is inviting and hospitable. As far as it is in your control, give thought to the size of the room, so that you meet in a place neither so small as to be smothering, nor too large and non-embracing. It should be simply but comfortably furnished and arranged so as to inspire confidence while at the same time offering a real sense of peaceful acceptance. Offer the seeker a warm and non-threatening welcome; ensure that the room has good lighting, is comfortably warm, and that you have cut yourself off from all sources of unwanted interruption or distraction.

The listener must be able to retain confidences; these should be broken only with the seeker's permission if additional advice is needed. The listener must be clear about their own limitations, including availability of time.

Take care before interrupting, or interjecting with one's own story or with experiences that may or may not be helpful. Avoid fatigue by providing necessary space between each seeker's visit. I generally take a 30 to 45 minute break between sessions, time for letting go of the previous seeker's story.

Be at peace within yourself; be genuine; be your own person. Be attentive. Be careful when offering advice, especially prematurely. Be aware of the importance of the relationship; be aware of any judgemental attitudes; be aware of racism, fundamentalism, sexism, feminism and any other 'ism' that may be lurking around. Be aware of key words and how they are used. Be very clear about boundaries; be realistic about how much you are able to cope with.

Having a good practice and policy for reviewing the way you feel about the encounter will help to identify characteristic ways you feel about yourself:

- How do your feelings facilitate or interfere with your involvement with others in your personal and/or your professional life?
- What fears and anxieties do you have that may prevent you listening attentively to the seeker?
- How do you quieten your inner fears and anxieties?
- How do you prevent yourself from being judgemental or rejecting of self and others?
- How may you be prevented from being an attentive listener who hears?

2
Hearing to listen

A wise old owl lived in an oak,
The more he saw the less he spoke.
The less he spoke the more he heard;
Why can't we all be like that bird?

Nursery rhyme quoted by Anthony Bloom,
Meditations on a Theme, p. 37

To listen, according to the *Shorter Oxford Dictionary*, is 'to hear attentively, to give ear, to make an effort to hear something'. It is not a passive affair, a space where we happen not to be doing or saying anything. It is a conscious, willed action, requiring alertness and vigilance, by which our whole attention is focused and controlled. So it is difficult. But what is hearing? I suggest it is the most natural activity for initiating empathy, understanding and acceptance. It is the activity that puts me in touch, when I am most attentively alert, even with that which is unsaid and perhaps even unsayable. In this situation even silence has its own voice, to be heard by the listener and seeker alike.

Most people are not aware precisely how and when hearing begins. If we knew, we might take better care of this wonderful gift. In his book *The Conscious Ear*, which records his important research in sound, learning and health, Aelfred A. Tomatis describes how 'the ear, foetus-shaped is able to function from four and half months after conception' (Tomatis, *The Conscious Ear*, p. 144). He writes:

> our investigations showed not only that the foetus hears, but also that it knows how to listen because it is capable of integrating sounds. We established that the embryo, from the second month of life in the womb, is able to sort out the

data that reach in at the level of vestibule-cochlear nuclei. At this point of development the birth of primitive memory takes place (*usually occurring less than thirty-seven weeks after conception*) which later will be diffused throughout the nervous system as it pursues its own much slower development than that of the auditory organism. So the embryo-foetus as far as listening is concerned, is born, giving a glimpse of structures being prepared that lead to the human being, by implication already alive and vibrant since the moment of conception. (ibid., pp. 209–10)

The author has so much to tell us about the mysteries of hearing that it is worth while taking the time to read the whole book. This last quotation sums up for me the reason why what he has to say is important. He writes,

Listening leads the foetus towards assuming its task of becoming a human being. Listening calls not only the ear, *but also* on the whole coetaneous sensitivity, even deep visceral sensitivity. It means stretching out one's whole body to the other in order to listen, but it is also to confront one's own existence by means of the same relationship. It is impossible to listen without involving oneself, and listening begins with one's own self-listening in the organising of relationships. (ibid., p. 215)

Throughout my life I have grown, and continue to grow, into the ways of hearing through being listened to and heard by others and, equally, through inviting seekers to comment on or challenge my listening, my hearing and my attentiveness. Does the seeker feel I am with him during our time of sharing? This hearing through listening to the other person demands a great deal of silence, which can so often be more powerful than words. It is through the silences of someone who is crying out to be heard and yet who is unable to vocalise for some reason, that our listening can offer help.

Hearing is about listening beyond words to the silences within and around them. When I read, if attentive, I am able to hear the silent word emanating through the word, sentence or passage, causing me to stop and allow it to speak to me. I feel this is similar to what happens through being in the silence of meditation or standing in the wonder of the sunrise or sunset, in the wonder of nature, in the wonder of the other person or myself. Through such listening, I am reminded how central the differing modes of hearing are to my growth, physically and spiritually.

The hearing person as a successful listener will not engage in dispute with other listeners, their theories or practice of listening; will regard his way of listening as being only one of many ways, thus recognising and accepting the uniqueness of each seeker and listener; will not regard his own beliefs, attitudes or opinions as equally appropriate for the seeker. It is for the seeker, not the listener, to decide whether and how his beliefs, attitudes and opinions should or should not change. The listener will accept the fact that he does not know what is best for the seeker. He is not the seeker and he will not be afraid to admit this.

The listener, where appropriate, will reveal to the seeker his own vulnerability, but not in such a way as to cause the seeker/listener roles to be reversed. Where appropriate, he will reveal to the seeker his beliefs, attitudes and opinions, thereby enabling the seeker to be aware of and to deal with the listener's biases and prejudices. The listener will not manipulate the seeker into becoming a credit to himself as a listener. Rather he will accept and support where possible the decisions the seeker makes about his life in becoming a credit to himself. The listener, through hearing, empowers the seeker to hear his own decisions from deep within, and to act upon them. The listener will not hide behind jargon, receptionists and rigid appointment systems. He will not act out the role of being constantly warm and embracing. Through his integrity of purpose he is prepared to simply be alongside the seeker and be his own wounded self, open to the wounds of the seeker.

There is little doubt that hearing within the silences of life has, through the centuries, inspired all the differing faiths, as shown in the Old Testament, the New Testament and the Koran. All three books are full of exhortations and instructions about silence, listening, hearing and responding. Hearing is referred to no fewer than 91 times within the first five books of the Old Testament. The first mention of hearing comes in the Book of

Genesis, 'and they heard the voice of the Lord! (Gen. 3:8)', while in the last book of the New Testament we read 'The Spirit and the Bride say, "Come!" And let those who hear say, "Come!" ' (Rev. 22:17). The Psalms proclaim, 'Today you will hear his voice' (Ps. 95:8), and 'Cause me to hear thy loving kindnesses in the morning' (Ps. 143:8); but they conclude, 'They have ears, but they hear not' (Ps. 115:6). In the Koran, the Prophet says, 'My Lord knows what is said in heaven and on earth; God is all-hearing and all-knowing' (Cleary, *Essential Koran*, p. 74).

Hearing with the 'fourth ear'

We can perhaps think again of the 'four in one' of hearing. The first ear listens to myself, the second ear to the other, the third to the silences and space behind words. Hearing with the fourth ear takes me out to the wider community and enables me to become more aware of the political and spiritual content within what is being shared between seekers.

Hearing with the 'fourth ear' demands that at best, I have the ability to wait with the courage of faith, to be gentle with myself and the seeker who comes with the hope that I have the time and the ability to remain in the quietness of the mystery, to wait with her through the voices of silence. For this, I need to become acutely aware of the shift from listening to hearing, as our focusing comes in line with each other at depth: as mind meets with mind; as feelings meet with feelings; as body meets with body; as soul meets with soul. As total persons meet with each other with the integrity of respect, spelling out that we are being confidentially and uniquely to each other in our shared sacredness, sharing our vulnerability and our co-creative potential for mutual growth.

Hearing with the fourth ear enables me to realise I do not have all the answers, that at times I am limited, with a restricted range of sympathies, differing depths of compassion and empathy. I am more open to hearing when I realise my own imperfections and when I do not take myself too seriously. I cultivate through my integrity of purpose a knowledge of when to call upon others and when to guide the seeker towards other sources that may meet her needs rather than my own. Unless, with the help of others, I expand my fourth ear, I will not be alert as to when best to encourage the seeker to become more aware and open to her potential for growth. This in-depth alertness is crucial in encouraging the release of the healing and growth energies inherent in every person.

Hearing through listening with the fourth ear enables me to become acutely aware of how I have been, systematically and to a certain extent institutionally, shaped by the conditions in which I have lived and moved towards the truth of my becoming. In order to achieve this awareness I will have looked at the emotional, intellectual, social and spiritual aspects of my life and that of the seeker. I cannot look at and listen to these without also looking at and listening to the external forces that are either co-creative or co-destructive within both the seeker and myself.

Listening with the in-depth hearing of the fourth ear is essential if I am to encourage change. The expanding of the fourth ear enables me to hear and call for other resources beyond my capabilities, if perhaps the seeker or myself feel we are unsuitable to each other for the necessary work to be done with confidence. We will not be able to encourage change in society unless we have previously spent time uncovering our own feelings about power and authority; about our maleness and femaleness; about our gender-related assumptions and expectations; and about varying lifestyles and differing spiritualities. Unless we have the courage, the hope and the faith to allow for the unending expansion of our hearing via the fourth ear we shall not be able to hear or feel the pain of the seeker who is experiencing a sense of rejection, of being cast out by others, family or the community, its secular or religious groups.

Any person seeking a listener who hears is saying 'I need to change', through being encouraged and supported in such a way that she feels she is accepted. The expanding act of hearing through listening via the fourth ear acts like a radar system – it is extremely sensitive to all that is being said or not said. As an expanding listener, I am prepared to be an advocate for the common good, yet with a committed concern for the individual. The expanding ear is the political and spiritual ear, concerned with issues of reconciliation between persons and groups; with the development of differing work and recreational facilities; with environmental issues that are endangering all living creatures, humanity, the ecosystem, and indeed the whole cosmic system;

with issues of releasing myself and others to achieve their greatest potential as co-inhabitants with co-responsibilities towards each other, all living creatures and the earth that is our mutual home.

The difficulties of hearing the anger of depression

Richie, my partner and companion for twenty years, suffered from recurring depression. He showed me how difficult it can be to hear the needs of a person suffering from deep depression. I remember attempting to care for him in the depths of a reactive depression, rooted in the loss of work which led to a loss of self-esteem, and in turn confirmed in him a deeper sense of worthlessness. This was all complicated by a lack of understanding as to the real reason for the depression. It was as though he was grieving for himself. At the same time it seemed to weaken our ability to communicate, and his ability to do anything for himself or anyone else. At times he had hardly the strength of will to move from A to B, however short the distance.

Although I was aware of all the circumstances of Richie's depression, this did not prevent me from becoming very angry with him at times, unable to hear and be with him. This may have been due to my own anxieties, neither understood nor cleared. I had not heard, or perhaps had not paid enough attention to, my own need for help in times of rejection and loss. And I was also angry with him because I felt so vulnerable in my helplessness. All I could do was 'be there', as a reference point to his value as a person with a real future.

Though one can never truly feel another person's pain – it is uniquely his or hers – I could sense his pain in the silences we shared. I could also feel my own pain and my need to be heard. I needed to be freed from my own pain and to talk with my 'soul friend' about my sense of helplessness and frustration. This discussion enabled me to release my pain, thus freeing myself. I was then better able to hear Richie's feelings of being lost, that he was of no value to himself or anyone else. Lost in his dark sea of depression, his ability grew to understand the 'why'. Gradually, in his own time, nurtured by the warmth of acceptance and the growing inner light of hope which strengthened his innate potential for healing, he was able to return to work.

The hearing of others begins with hearing myself; similarly, the loving of others begins with loving myself. This is the beginning of my love for others and the fulfilling of the great command- ment that we shall 'love God and our neighbour as ourselves' (Luke 10:27). Listening to ourselves means that we listen to our- selves rightly. Most of us love ourselves too much or too little; we are selfish or feel totally worthless. When we listen to our- selves we hear that we are loved, and can be loving of others. We believe that 'fear of the Lord is the beginning of wisdom' (Ps. 111:10); the beginning of being fully alive to all and everything around and within ourselves.

Aids to Effective Hearing
Caring for the care-taker

Caring for oneself is perhaps the hardest lesson to learn for those who are committed to caring for others. I cannot be there for other people unless I am being there for myself. It is so tempting to want to be there, to be 'on call' if not 'on duty'. I must not be afraid to look after myself and recognise that I also need to accept and receive care and attention from others, including those I myself have cared for.

Karl Barth says of God that he 'gives himself, but he does not give himself away'. Seen in this light, 'taking up one's cross' takes on a new meaning. It is not the denial of our true selves, but knowing ourselves to be valued, and in valuing ourselves that we reach out for the sake of others. It is a free choice, a con- sent to the seemingly inevitable, rather than a destruction of 'self'. It is a self-respect that is generous, both in self-giving and in a refusal to forsake one's own humanity, even in desperate circumstances. 'God gives himself, but he does not give himself away – he does not cease to be God' (Mann, *A Double Thirst*, p. 78). Therefore I too should never cease to become fully Bill, fully myself.

As a listener, my responsibility is to prevent any harmful exposure of my inner sanctuary, my soul, not only for my own protection but also as a service to those who come into my orbit of concern. I am aware that just as words lose their power when they are not born out of silence, so openness loses its meaning when there is no desire for self-care.

Caring for self demands that I be acutely aware of the baggage I carry, from the views I have received via my family and background, the media, newspapers and journals I read, to those of friends and mentors, the influence of my teachers, my culture, and the stories of the many who come to see me. There is no point in caring for others unless one has an *adequate sense* of one's own need for self-caring. It is crucial that one learns to protect oneself from being sucked dry; to draw on the spiritual, the non-material resources, available so that one is sufficiently replenished to continue caring for the seeker.

> In seeking to relieve the needs of others we seek to give ourselves, *but not to give ourselves away*. We cannot serve humanity if we lose our own humanity. The task is to be our selves and reach beyond our selves, becoming truly eccentric – out of centre – centred in God but reaching beyond ourselves. In this way we not only respect ourselves but offer true respect for others, for we recognise our own connectedness but also our distinctiveness.
>
> (Mann, *A Double Thirst*, p. 122)

Be a resource to yourself. If you never say 'No', what is your 'Yes' worth? Caring for oneself is being able to 'let go'. This does not mean we stop caring; it means acknowledging that if we cannot care for ourselves, how can we care for someone else? To let go is not to cut oneself off; it is the realisation that you cannot control another. To let go is not to enable, but to allow oneself to learn from natural consequences. To let go is to admit powerlessness; it is to recognise that the outcome is not in my hands. To let go is not to try to change or blame another; it is to make the most of myself. To let go is not to care for, but to care about. To let go is not to fix, but to be supportive. To let go is not to judge, but to allow another to be a human being. To let go is not to be in the middle arranging all the outcomes, but to allow others to affect their destinies. To let go is not to be protective; it is to permit another to face reality. To let go is not to deny, but to accept. To let go is not to scold, nag or argue, but instead to search out my own shortcomings and correct them. To let go is not to adjust everything to my desires, but to take each day as it comes and cherish myself in it. To let go is not to criticise or regulate anybody, but to try to become what I could be. To let go is not to regret the past, but to grow and live for the future. To let go is to fear less and love more. To let go is to live in the 'now' moments of our lives.

Caring for myself demands that I accept the need for relationships that are close and strong in their support of me, Bill, thereby enabling me to be available to myself before others. The experience of this deeply supportive network is the experience of our basic human needs.

One of the many ways of caring for oneself is to take time for brief periods of relaxation of two to three minutes throughout the day. The following can be helpful:

- Sitting comfortably in a chair, leaning back if possible, and keeping your neck supported, with feet and legs relaxed, close your eyes (finish reading these instructions first, though!). Count backwards from three to one, taking a deep breath with each count. Breathe in through your nose and breathe out through your mouth. Make sure you are breathing from the diaphragm and then the upper chest.
- Scan your body mentally to find tense spots (clenched jaw, tight shoulders, etc.) and relax them as much as possible.
- Rotate your head slowly in a circular motion, once or twice in each direction. Slowly roll your shoulders backwards and forwards, twice in each direction.
- Conjure up a pleasant thought, memory, feeling or image for a few seconds longer.
- Take one more deep breath, exhale slowly and then return to work!

There are also a number of more general ways in which we can care for ourselves. These include:

- Be gentle with yourself. Remind yourself that you are an enabler, not a magician. We cannot change anybody else. We can only change how we relate to them.
- Find your own special spot and use it daily.
- In giving support, encouragement and praise to colleagues and others, learn to accept it in return. Remember that in the light of all the pain we see, we are bound to feel helpless at

times. Admit it without shame. More often than not, caring and 'being there' are more important than doing.

- Change your routine often, and your tasks when you can.
- Learn to recognise the difference between complaining that relieves, and complaining that reinforces negative stress.
- On the way home, focus on one good thing that occurred during the day.

Thoughts on impaired hearing

During the long gestation of the writing of this book, I gave little thought to the problems of those with varying degrees of impaired hearing. I had met many people whose lip-reading was so good that I was unaware of their severe hearing impairment. This has changed since my own hearing became impaired. Initially I found it difficult to believe this was happening. Friends and others began to ask me, 'Are you going deaf?' My reply in the early years was always 'No'. Eventually I became more and more aware of the fact that while watching television I had to keep turning the sound up. Finally I saw my GP, who promptly arranged an appointment for me to see an audio therapist. Initially, I asked myself, how was I going to make up for the loss of my hearing, realising that the impairment would not decrease but rather the reverse. Apart from taking lip-reading lessons, I would need to rely on the four remaining senses of seeing, smelling, touching and tasting, each of which would come into play at the right time.

Verena Tschudin reminds us that hearing is 'crucial in our understanding of life. We become aware through listening – with our ears and our hearts', and, I believe, with our souls. 'The senses are the go-between physical and spiritual, between material and mental understanding; between compassion and empathy' (Tschudin, *Hearing Ourselves*, p. 13). I believe that they also make the connection between heaven and earth; between our inner and outer selves; between the positive and negative forces. They all bring these worlds together. Their message, here as everywhere, is listen and hear, 'something which has existed since the beginning, that we have heard, and we have seen with out own eyes; that we have watched and touched with our hands: the Word, who is life – this is our subject' (John 1:1). (Tschudin, *Hearing Ourselves*, p. 13)

Aids for helping a hearing-impaired person understand you

When someone speaks, clues are gained not only from what is heard but also from what is seen. These clues complement and supplement each other, helping the hearing-impaired person to piece together the conversation For such people the visual clues of speech are very important. Simple actions on your part may determine the ease with which these visual clues can be followed. The following points will help:

- Attract the observer's attention before you start talking to them so they can catch the beginning of what is said and not just the ending.
- Avoid speaking from another room, or with your head in a cupboard.
- Keep your face visible and ensure it is well lit.
- Try to avoid conversation in the kitchen where there may be background sound from food mixers, washing machines, dishwashers, etc.
- Do not hide your lip movements behind your hands, a cigarette, a pipe or a paper.
- Do not speak while looking into a newspaper or book.
- Keep your head fairly still while speaking.
- Use natural hand gestures but do not exaggerate.
- Do not shout – speak clearly and not too fast; shouting and over-enunciating will alter the lip pattern, while speaking too slowly may destroy the natural rhythm of speech.
- Try to make the subject of conversation as clear as possible.
- Try to use full sentences rather than short phrases, as they are easier to understand.
- For a person with impaired hearing it is important to see the speaker's eyes to gauge how they are feeling. Therefore if you are wearing sunglasses remove these while speaking.
- Repeat the sentence again if necessary and then perhaps rephrase what you want to say. You may not be aware of this but some words are more difficult to lip-read than others; for example, the month 'March' is easier to lip-read than

'August'. In the word 'March' the shapes making the 'm' and 'ch' are visible on the lips, but the components of 'August' are made inside the mouth so there is nothing to see.

- Write down any important facts.
- Remember that a hearing aid amplifies background noise as well as speech.

The following are the best conditions for listening to a hearing-impaired person:

- Use a room with soft furnishings (such as carpets, curtains and cushions, which absorb sound and so reduce the echo effect).
- Try to reduce background noise (a tablecloth may muffle the noise of clattering plates, for example).
- Ask others to face you, to speak clearly and just a little louder than normal (mumbling and shouting make it more difficult for you to pick out the words of the speaker).
- Remember that it will be rather more difficult to communicate in noisy places such as busy streets, large shops, hospitals, railways, aircraft and all large transport stations and airports because of the very loud background noise.

Aids for the hearing-impaired listener

For listeners whose own hearing is impaired, the following will make it easier to understand conversation:

- We must not be afraid to tell people that you are having difficulty in hearing.
- Make sure the room is well lit.
- Have your back to the light source, e.g. the window, so that the light falls on the speaker's face.
- Position yourself at a distance of three to six feet from the speaker, as lip-reading is difficult if the speaker is too near or too far away.
- Make sure your eyesight is regularly tested, as you don't want to strain your eyes.
- Try to watch the speaker's lips (you may be surprised at the number of clues you pick up without realising it).

- Do not let yourself get too tired or tense, as you will be able to lip-read better if you are relaxed.
- Do not be afraid to let people know that you have to rely to some extent on lip-reading, and give them an idea of how they can help you.

3

Creative listening

When two or more people share a profound silence they bestow healing on one another

Donald Nichol

Creative listening is essentially a method for use between the seeker and the listener. It developed out of the realisation, most clearly articulated by Dr Rachel Pinney, that a person cannot give full attention to what is being said to them while at the same time assessing it and framing a reply. Dr Pinney writes: 'I cannot do this and nor can anyone else I have met. *True listening rarely occurs.*' The process begins when the seeker, having sought assistance, is given an explanation by the listener of this method of listening, and is then invited to take part. It is a method that makes space and time for both participants to speak, the seeker and listener usually alternating for three minutes at a time throughout a 45 to 50 minute session. It is helpful to have available a clock with a soft-sounding alarm or an egg timer, preferably placed where it may be heard or seen by both persons.

The listener chooses at what point to summarise and reflect, and may interrupt so as to prevent the seeker from saying too much during one period (although, as in all things, there may be exceptions). This is essential if the summary is to be effective in the reflections it offers; if the seeker continues to speak for too long without a break, it is hard for the listener to maintain the concentration necessary to offer an effective summary. Both listener and seeker may also interrupt in order to gain clarification on a point not fully understood or heard. Just before the end of the allotted finishing time, the listener will offer an overall recap.

Recapping is not a parrot-like repetition of the seeker's words;

on the other hand it is important that the listener should refrain from making any comment, value judgement, or 'helpful' suggestion. It is equally important for the listener to employ the seeker's own idiom, thereby making it clear to the seeker that he or she has not only been heard but also understood. For example:

> Seeker: I've just had a terrible row with my boss, he treats me like a slave to his every whim – he constantly asks why he should keep me on the staff even though I am his senior office manager in front of my team.
> Listener: You are feeling bad after a quarrel with your boss, who does not appreciate you.

There is no doubt that any movement of the seeker towards the potential listener is an act of courage. A person who decides to listen as an 'act of will' has given the decision and its consequences some attention. In using the creative listening method this 'act of will' is made at the start, before the listening takes place. I would suggest that the same is true of the seeker who has made 'an act of will' to speak. These 'acts of will' having been made, the listener is able to offer his or her full potential as a listener towards the full potential of the seeker by adopting some simple procedures. With practice this enables almost everyone to achieve 'single attention', or what Buddhists call 'mindfulness'.

Whatever our views of the seeker, and however great the urge to interrupt, it is important to let them speak. The creative listening method entails the listener switching off her own views for the duration of the listening period, in the awareness that 'we cannot offer our full attention to what is being said and at the same time be assessing it and framing a reply.' By switching off, the listener is able to offer total attention to the seeker. In the process, she will have a brand new experience: by not interrupting or arguing with the seeker, the listener will hear stories never heard before.

I believe that nearly all of those who are involved in the stillness of listening will agree that our prime gift is to 'be there' with the seeker, to abandon anything that might affect our listening potential. It is natural that if, throughout our lives, we offer ourselves to be heard and at the same time pay attention, this will teach us how to listen, to be totally present to the seeker, in such a way that the seeker is able to hear himself from deep within. In this sense, listener and seeker are being co-creative through their co-listening to each other.

Pastoral Listening

Listening by pastors or priests and lay people within the Church is known as pastoral listening. It is spirituality in action on behalf of the seeker. I believe that the basic message of pastoral care is that people matter. This is linked to our feeling secure in ourselves, that we matter in our own right and in relationship to others, and that others matter to us. Pastoral care is recognising and assisting the seeker to locate the mystery of God within.

Like love, spirituality cannot easily be defined. The word has a long and varied history. Along with words like love, soul and God, it holds no allegiance to one single group, culture or religion. For me, true spirituality is the embracing of all life and creation. It is the inner lifeblood of the world, and nothing is separated from it. Through our Creator we are all brothers and sisters to each other, all the sons and daughters of God. As it is in heaven, so on earth. There is no separation, we are all webbed together for all eternity.

Kurtz and Ketcham, the founders of Alcoholics Anonymous, coined the phrase 'The spirituality of imperfection'. They write that 'the spirituality of imperfection is thousands of years old' (Kurtz and Ketcham, *The Spirituality of Imperfection*, p. 2). It is a 'spirituality of why we are? How are we to live?' (ibid., p. 7). 'The spirituality is based on the lived experience of acceptance of human limitations and powerlessness' (ibid., p. 6). Spirituality itself is conveyed by stories, using words that go beyond words to speak the language of the heart and soul. Especially in a spirituality of imperfection, a spirituality of not having all the answers, stories convey the mystery and the miracle of every life, nurtured by the adventure of being alive.

This can be clearly seen and heard when seekers dare to reveal the story of their lives, their imperfections and their needs. In so doing they may very well remind us of our own needs and imperfections. Hopefully we will be aware of these imperfections within us and will be able to detach ourselves from them when listening to the seeker's stories. If we have not done so, we shall be unable to hear the person of the seeker.

> What is absolutely fundamental to a pastoral style is the understanding that most people are responsible for their own unique inner world, and that no one else can save them from themselves. The aim of pastoral listening is to assist the seeker to take this responsibility seriously. This means that pastoral listeners must recognise their limits and be equipped with the knowledge of who indeed may be best suited to help a person come to terms with what is needed. Pastoral listening refers to a listening that centres on the inner world i.e. the spiritual life of the person. It is the ability to listen with care and with an educated ear, so that the individual can be assisted to take personal responsibility for whatever problem is exposed.
>
> (Moran, *Listening*, pp. 4–65)

Pastoral listening is not a passive affair; it is a willed action requiring alertness and vigilance that is focused and controlled. One attempts to be there for the seeker, who desires to be treated as someone who matters.

Some seek out a priest in the expectation that he or she will allow them to pour out their innermost thoughts and feelings, or will have more time for them, while enabling them to feel safe due to the priest's covenant of confidentiality. Some turn to a priest in the belief that she is a representative of God; it is assumed that God will be listening and will respond to their needs. From 1975 to 1978 I was a novice member of the Society of St Francis. After I left the Franciscans, a work colleague asked me if I was going to start wearing my clerical collar again. She hoped not. 'Why not continue wearing your habit?' she continued. 'There is such an obvious difference between the priest and the friar. I always feel that monks and nuns are less judgemental. They take you as you are; they let you know in a more gentle way that you are acceptable just as you are, warts and all.' For her, the clerical collar spoke of restriction and judgement, while the habit spoke of acceptance and freedom.

I suggest that spirituality releases the art of transformation.

When the seeker arrives with his worries and pains, he is seeking assistance towards changes with regard to a particular situation, trusting that these will occur through an understanding of the 'why' of his need to be heard. And over time change will occur.

As a pastoral listener, I have been involved with people who state, 'I have a problem. Have you a minute?' This usually means, 'I'm in pain, will you relieve me of it?' When I was working at Centrepoint, in Soho, I lived over the night shelter, and as I was going up to bed, a volunteer or staff member might often ask, 'Have you a minute?' That minute would become a half hour due to some personal problem in the person's family that had to be shared immediately. The listener cannot take on the work that rightly belongs to the seeker. Those in need will sometimes attempt to hand over responsibility to anyone who will listen and relieve them of their anxieties, but if we were to take on the seeker's responsibility, we would be diminishing the responsibility that is rightly theirs, and diminishing their potential for growth.

This has awakened in me the awareness that I am not a person who has a spiritual being, but rather I am a spiritual being who lives and has human experiences. Being heard through our imperfections is part of the spiritual process towards healing and is essential for human growth. Being heard in depth enables the seeker to hear, from within her own depth, an answer to the problem or situation. Through having been heard, the seeker may receive a glimpse of what the power of both darkness and light can offer from the depths and the heights of the unknown. The role of the pastoral listener is one that is constantly being nurtured by the ability to hear and identify at a deeper level with the needs of the seeker.

One of the practical advantages offered by a pastoral listener is that they are often the first person available to deal with an immediate crisis, especially when other caring personnel are not readily available. However, it is important not to try to be all things to all people. To do so may create problems not only for the listener, but also for the seeker. I believe that every seeker who comes into my presence arrives carrying the unique personal story of their journey. It takes courage on the part of the seeker, who is wondering what the listener will think. Will there be acceptance or rejection? Will I be listened to and heard, affirmed or not?

Throughout my listening ministry I am constantly being made aware that I can never assume to know the all of the seeker. I am aware that behind every new revelation, there is a further mystery hidden within the 'cloud of unknowing'. I am aware that both the seeker and myself are on similar, though different, journeys and that it needs care by the listener not to confuse the two journeys.

Whenever I am asked to see someone new, I seek as little information as possible from the person making the request. I want to meet this new person with as clear a mind as possible; labels tend to cloud the mind, as does any brief history. This approach allows the seeker the freedom to choose to be for himself rather than for me, and perhaps it will allow him to drop any self-labelling that may be imprisoning him. This kind of detachment is offered with the dignity of respect for the uniqueness of the person.

Pastoral listening, as spirituality in action on behalf of the seeker, recognises and assists the seeker to locate the mystery of self within, no matter why or how this person presents herself. Spirituality, like love, is the way we behave towards ourselves and the other person. I have come to realise that our spiritualities cannot be pinned down in religion. Both demand the freedom of liberation. I believe that the seeker, consciously or unconsciously, is seeking the right to evolve into the true reality of self and that this may include a new image of God as the ultimate Mother and Father of us all, who have, with their own DNA, seeded each person into the mystery of life. It's all so very awesome that only in the silences of being with, and for, each other can we even begin to grasp the wonder, the mystery of every life and all of creation.

Soul Listening

> To 'listen' another's soul into a condition of disclosure and discovery may be almost the greatest service any human being ever performs for another
>
> *Douglas V. Steere,* Gleanings, *p. 45*

I believe that to become involved in the ministry of 'soul listening' is to be aware that the soul is one of the most vulnerable aspects of one's total self. It is the centre of our encounter and experience with the Holy Mystery seeded within all persons. Cari Jackson in her book *The Gift to Listen, The Courage to Hear* writes:

> Listening is an 'inner-personal' activity. The effectiveness as a communicator begins within, by listening deeply to one's own soul. Listening is more than an aspect of communication, it is also a spiritual process ... To foster this kind of listening, I have developed what I call 'soul listening' techniques. Soul listening enables listeners to go beyond the interpersonal forces of active listening to the inner-personal. Soul listening uses spirituality based listening tools that can enable you to connect more deeply with others by deepening of your own feelings. With greater clarity about your feelings, you can hear what others are saying more clearly. (Jackson, *The Gift to Listen*, p. xi)

The author reminds us,

> Some form or other of listening as a spiritual practice is encouraged to varying degrees by different spiritual traditions. For example, in Islam, the importance of listening to God the creator is emphasised as the way to peace and well-being. In Judaism and Christianity the Wisdom of God is made available in human experience, but must be listened for, discerned, and interpreted carefully. In Zen Buddhism, the concept of listening deeply to others (as well as self) is stressed as part of right livelihood and living fully in each present moment. Taoist teaching centres on listening to and surrendering to the Tao, which results in giving up judgements and desires and in becoming more compassionate.
>
> (ibid., p. 4)

As we have said, listening is a skill that has to be learned, and the same is true of soul listening. It goes far beyond the ability to hear spoken words, but rather involves the qualities of 'the heart, the mind and the soul. It involves caring (the heart), intention (the mind) and courage (the soul)' (ibid., p. 45). I suggest it has also to do with meditation (the heart), prayer (the mind) and contemplation (the soul).

Spiritually, listening is a practice orientated towards soul listening. There is no doubt that, at best, each connection we make with the speaker is a starting point, an opportunity for both listener and speaker to love and learn, to grow in wisdom, and with practice to expand our differing abilities for hearing, accepting the innate dignity of the other person and ourselves. This allows us to expand the sphere of our soul – listening in order to embrace others, the all of humanity, Mother Earth and the cosmos towards the One all-inclusive, all-embracing Relationship with God.

Meditation and mindful listening

The Zen master promotes meditation as a way of emptying the mind of clutter and unproductive thoughts, making space for personal growth. Meditation allows our minds to hear less distortion, letting in new ideas and points of view. Regular meditation practice improves our attitudes and the ability to offer our attention, and sets the scene for mindful listening. It costs us no money and the great joy is that it is free of religious bias. It is the most natural way of connecting oneself to new ways of thinking and listening; the calmness of an open mind, and focused attention, are the very foundation for both mindful and attentive listening, whether to self or others.

During my periods of meditation, I do not work at avoiding the thoughts that skip through my mind. I simply recognise their presence and let them pass by through re-focusing on my breathing. Regular breathing in our periods of meditation helps us to restore balance and the connection between body, mind and soul. It nurtures our connection with the self, with others and with differing communities. In learning how to improve our breathing, from tight, shallow breathing towards deep abdominal breathing, we relax our neck and our shoulders. We may not see or feel instant results, but over several days or maybe a few weeks, the changes will become apparent.

It is well known that meditation increases the brain's alpha waves and will elevate our sense of well-being. It can also be used as a means of promoting inner peace, a means to gain a sense of deep relaxation, thereby allowing us to step back from situations and see them in a clearer light, unobstructed by barriers and noise. Eventually, through regular practice, this relaxation will begin to permeate every cell of our body and each interaction.

My early morning practice is generally along these lines, as I prepare myself for growing attentively into the silence of just being in the mystery of awesomeness that embraces my life. Having performed my ablutions, washing my face and hands, I have a cup of hot lemon or green tea, without sugar or honey. I begin my period of meditation or contemplation having prepared my space, sitting on a comfortable chair with a tall hard back to keep my spine and neck in a straight line, relaxed, with my feet on the floor, usually without socks. I rest my hands, palms facing upwards, on my thighs. In doing this, I like to think I am being mindful and receptive to the differing energies that may be nurturing this time of reaching in, that I may reach out more fruitfully.

Like most of us when entering periods of prayer, embraced in the deeper silence, we may find ourselves becoming more meditative, and eventually flowing into contemplation through simply 'being there' in the midst of the mystery surrounding our lives and the all of creation. I used to believe quite strongly that action took precedence over times of prayer. It was while working at Centrepoint in Soho that I eventually realised that, on the contrary, prayer should be the priority because it has the power to nurture us and our daily activities, for our own selves as much as for others.

Thich Nhat Hanh, in *Peace is Every Step*, says: 'When we want to understand something, we cannot just stand outside and observe it. We have to enter deeply into it and be one with it in order to really understand' (quoted in Jackson, *The Gift to Listen*, p. ix). 'The lesson we must learn is that love is to listen.'

> *A Way Out of No Way*
> We must lend ears to the songs
> and signs of life found in nature,
> the events of history, and social encounters
> of our daily routine

We never know when or how new meaning
Might break through.
> (Andrew Young, *A Way Out of No Way*, p. 65)

Walking the labyrinth

Labyrinths are to be found in religious traditions all over the
world. Many take the form of a large circle, with a single wind-
ing path that leads through four quadrants to the centre. They
became established in the Catholic Church during the crusades,
when pilgrimages to the Holy Land were dangerous, and people
needed another way of honouring their vows. During a visit to
San Francisco, I walked into Grace Cathedral, simply to look
around and enjoy a meditative period of 'just being' before the
humbling mystery of silence. When I saw the labyrinth there, I
sat down and watched three or four people walking it in a very
meditative manner. I did not myself walk the labyrinth on that
particular visit but within a couple of days, at differing times, I
did make the journey. The first time I came away gently moved
and refreshed; the second time I felt an embracing presence and
a sense of being between here and there, especially while in the
middle of the labyrinth.

One of the main features of the labyrinth journey is that it
appeals to seekers of all faiths as well as those with little or no
faith background. I believe that hidden within the mystery of the
doubting seeker is an indefinable spirituality linked to that of
the labyrinth.

> There is no doubt that we are all labyrinth carriers – this is
> reflected in the inner landscape – the labyrinth of our inner
> ear, the coiling surfaces of the brain, the loops of our small
> intestine. It also symbolises the interior realms of the
> imagination and intuition, and the spiralling journey of
> reflection and meditation – the return to the deep source
> within. What we find there may be consciously integrated
> into our being to transform the way we are in the world;
> thus the labyrinth journey takes us inward but also back
> again to the ordinary reality of our everyday lives.
> (Fisher, p. 32)

Mark Barrett writes:

> We travel through the labyrinth by weaving a path of recur-
> sive arcs, and as we do the relentless demands of the many
> dimensions of our lives can be lifted from our shoulders.
> We move more naturally, because we no longer hurry – the
> turning about and about makes it pointless to rush frantic-
> ally forward. It can seem that we are carried on the slowly
> swirling waters of a great stream which turns and eddies as
> we travel: a lazy moment which travels not onwards but
> down, and supported in this slowly turning pool we can
> feel safe to our experience and our physical presence.
>
> (Barrett, *Crossing*, p. 69)

The more interested I become in this spiritual practice, the more
aware I am that walking the labyrinth is to walk in the ways of
the holy. I was reminded by a friend of a story in 1 Kings, where
King David is lying on his death bed talking to his son, Solomon.
David tells Solomon to be strong and courageous, and to walk in
the ways of God. To walk in the ways of the Holy requires that
you be strong in your inner self; that you equip yourself with
truth, justice and courage; and that you be constant in prayer,
alert and willing to persevere.

> The labyrinth is a valuable tool for considering the middle
> stage of the Christian journey ... One who wants to pray the
> labyrinth needs only to step onto the path and begin. This
> walking prayer is a gentle dance that requires no special
> skills or movements that call attention to themselves. The
> labyrinth allows the one who walks it to pray with the body,
> to be aware of the interplay of limbs and movement
> through space. In a way that threatens no one, we are
> allowed to experience ourselves as physical beings in a
> physical space. Our bodies are the vehicles and the means
> of our prayer – the cerebral nature of some prayer forms is
> helplessly side-stepped allowing dimensions of ourselves to
> come into prayer which might otherwise be left at the
> church door. (ibid., pp. 67, 69)

Lauren Artress informs us that in her experience, 'People in the labyrinth seem to gravitate to what I have come to call a process meditation. This meditation moves between silence and image, so that the focus does not remain solely on quieting the mind as in contemplative practice. This meditation also uses what is very close to a guided imagery process as a source of revelation' (Artress, *Walking a Sacred Path*, p. 77).

It has been suggested to me that some who are involved in listening to others seem to find it easier if they walk the labyrinth more quickly. Others who are stressed walk it to de-stress themselves. Often people who lead very busy lives deliberately set themselves, in response to their inner voice, to walk at a measured pace to slow themselves down. Research on the benefits of walking the labyrinth is still in its early stages, but I believe it will become recognised as an important healing tool. 'They provide the sacred space where inner and outer worlds convene, where thinking and the imaginative heart can flow together. It provides a space to listen to our inner voice of wisdom' (Fisher, p. 33).

In walking the labyrinth we are opening, inviting the flow of the Holy Spirit into our lives. Artress writes:

> The church is struggling with the issue of whether to address the Holy Spirit in the masculine or feminine. In my mind, there is no doubt that the Holy Spirit captures the essence of the feminine side of God. It is the cosmic openness, the receptive part of the Godhead that allows and understands the flow of our lives. It is the essence of God that helps us see our mistakes clearly, and transforms into building blocks for the next stage in our lives. She protects and guides us, is patient and merciful. This is the medieval understanding of Mary: the Mother of Jesus, Theotokos, the Mother of God, as embraced by the Eastern Church.
>
> (Artress, *Walking a Sacred Path*, pp. 161–2)

For this we need a new vision of what it means to be mature. 'The new vision of spiritual maturity is based on trust of inner wisdom and inner authority that has its moorings in a teaching tradition that guides us in the hard work of soul making' (ibid., p. 178). The beauty of the labyrinth motif is that its appeal is so multi-faceted. As a metaphor for life's journey, prompting us to think about the way we choose to travel the path – whether we savour each moment, secure in the belief that while life's problems will continue to challenge us, we have the inner resources and confidence to solve them, or whether we act like distracted onlookers, always wondering why someone else seems to have the better deal. Consciously walking the labyrinth can cause you to reflect on whether life is something that just happens to you, or is an experience with which you choose to truly engage. The labyrinth symbol can help you to reappraise your goals in life, to stop looking for a quick fix by latching on to this guru or that, and to accept full responsibility for your own spiritual enlightenment. After embracing the labyrinth as a metaphor for journeying into our deeper, hidden, authentic selves, many have been inspired to recognise that the source of contentment and wisdom lies within. Walking the labyrinth, consciously and with respect, has prompted others to ask themselves questions like these, and it is likely to do the same for you.

4

Compassion, empathy, dignity, mattering

*THE HOLY SPIRIT will never give you stuff
on a plate – you've got to work for it.
Your work is LISTENING – taking the situation
you're in and holding it in courage, not being beaten
down by it.
Your work is STANDING – holding things without
being deflected by your own desires or the
desires of other people round you. Then things
work out just through patience. How things
alter we don't know, but the situation alters.
There must be dialogue in patience and charity –
then something seems to turn up that wasn't
there before.
We must take people as they are and where they
are – not going too far ahead or too fast for
them, but listening to their needs and supporting
them in their following.
The Holy Spirit brings things new and old out of
the treasury.
Intercessors bring the 'deaf and dumb' to Christ
that is their part.
Seek for points of unity and stand on those rather
than on principles.
Have the patience that refuses to be pushed out;
the patience that refuses to be disillusioned.
There must be dialogue – or there will be no
development.*

Gilbert Shaw

Compassion

The word compassion is derived from the Latin words *pati* and *com*. Together, they mean 'to suffer with' those who are suffering. Compassion means to go where it hurts, into the places of pain, brokenness, fear, confusion and anguish. The Hebrew word for compassion expresses attachment of one person to another, i.e. between listener and seeker. When making this journey we are required to do so with sensitivity towards the sick, the vulnerable, the fearful and the outcast. It also demands of us action towards alleviating pain and suffering.

The compassionate way is also the way of *patie*nce. It is pure sensitivity, due to the fact that it touches the centre of our being human for ourselves and others, friend and non-friend alike. It certainly is not a feeling of pity, rather it is a genuine sense of responsibility. This responsibility stems from the ability to respond as best one is able. We are constantly responding, both to our own needs and to the needs of others. Every conversation is a response to words spoken, their implications, and the actions they evoke. If we respond to a person, we are expected to respond to the whole person. A person cannot be less of a person in one respect and more in another. We may not approve of certain acts by others (and ourselves) in certain situations but such acts make someone no less a person. And our response is to the 'whole' person. The depth of compassion for self releases our innate compassion towards others.

Compassion is caring, though it may also emphasise the mutuality of our weaknesses. When such caring is shown from out of two weaknesses, somehow by the grace of God strength is born. This paradox was beautifully illustrated by Michael Ramsey, former Archbishop of Canterbury, preaching in Canterbury Cathedral at the beginning of the 1988 Lambeth Conference:

> 'An arch', wrote Leonardo da Vinci, 'is nothing else than a strength caused by two weaknesses; for the arch in buildings is made up of two segments of a circle, and each of these segments, being itself very weak, desires to fall; and as one withstands the downfall of the other, the two weaknesses are converted into a single strength.'
>
> (Mann, *A Double Thirst*, pp. 87–8)

The twin arches of compassion and empathy encourage us to be weak with the weak, vulnerable with the vulnerable, powerless with the powerless, and hopeful with the hopeful; they mean full involvement in the work of becoming our being; for both seeker and listener alike, they refer to the very core of our deepest feelings; they are about non-smothering care and the maintenance of a 'bonding' rather than a 'binding' space between seeker and listener. Caring is liberated through the compassion of empathy. Henri Nouwen reminds us,

> The compassionate way is the patient way. Patience is the discipline of compassion. This becomes obvious when we realise that the word *compassion* could be read as *com-patience* [italics mine] ... The compassionate life could be described as a life patiently lived with others. If we then ask about the way of the compassionate life – about the discipline of compassion – patience is the answer. If we cannot be patient, we cannot be com-patient. If we ourselves are unable to suffer, we cannot suffer with others. If we lack the strength to carry the burden of our own lives, we cannot accept the burden of our neighbours. Patience is the hard but fruitful discipline of the disciple of the compassionate Lord. (Nouwen, McNeill, Morrison, *Compassion*, p. 92)

Empathy

The importance of empathic listening is well recognised and can be of great value in everyday situations. In any conversation the feeling that one has been heard and understood is a powerful statement of being acceptable, of having mattered. When the seeker realises that he has been heard and understood, there is no further need to prove his point of view or defend it against attack, and a feeling of quietness of mind and relaxation of the body follows, brought about by having let go of defensive behaviour.

Listeners are expected to be 'sensitive linkers', able to link into the seeker's vulnerability, wounds and pain, in such a manner as to liberate her innate healing energies. This ability is often grounded in the listener's own wounds, serious illnesses, traumas and all manner of other wounds, be they physical, mental, social, educational or spiritual. Seekers are nurtured by the fact that they have the courage of hope and a need to understand their wounds, and how this may enable them to become sources of healing. Most listeners have recognised and experienced their co-healing potential in that they have been gifted with the gift of empathy. Similarly, there must be empathy between the wounds of the seeker and the wounds of the listener. Clearly wounds do speak to wounds.

Mann offers us an important insight, quoting from Richie McMullen on the subject of 'my empathetic friend':

> 'My empathetic friend sees the unique mystery that is me. *Never fully understanding it* or deeply exploring it, he allows it to be' … '*Never fully understanding it*' reminds us not to assume that we can stand in someone else's shoes. Empathy is a willingness to see the world through their perception. It is also the ability to receive their communication with all our senses so that we understand more than the words alone convey. So we become fully engaged with their world, whilst recognising our distinctiveness in order to respect their individuality and our own – to make it possible to be fully there for them *because* we are distinct and not allowing ourselves to be overwhelmed by their pain (though, of course, at times we are deeply affected by it).
>
> (Mann, *A Double Thirst*, pp. 91–2)

Dignity

There appears to be a real lack of clarity concerning the meaning of the word dignity. A variety of definitions is offered in dictionaries, thesauruses, and the literature and journals designed for the professional and voluntary care services. This suggests to me that it is easier to talk about the idea of dignity than its meaning or practice. Dignity is the honouring of the distinct uniqueness of another person (and oneself), irrespective of how she presents herself at any given moment. It is innately demanded that we recognise, respect, affirm and honour the sacredness so often hidden behind differing labels, even those we give to ourselves; that we further recognise and honour each person's contribution to society, and are fearless in affirming the selfhood of any or all persons.

Seeking further clarification, I wrote to Dr Helen Oppenheimer – philosopher and former President of the Society for the Study of Christian Ethics – with this request: 'I would appreciate it if you would enlighten me further on the real meaning of the word "dignity" in relationship to care within the differing caring professions.' Her reply:

> I have found a quotation from Kant which seems relevant. He is talking about people as 'ends in themselves' and says: 'In the Kingdom of ends everything has either Value or Dignity. Whatever has a value can be replaced by something else that is equivalent; whatever, on the other hand, is above all value, and therefore admits of no equivalent, has Dignity.' ('Duties towards animals and spirits', in Kant's *Lectures in Ethics*. This is quoted in Mary Midgley, *Beast and Man*, Harvester Press, 1979, pp. 221–2, which is where I found it.)

I further asked myself, 'In the offering of respect am I not already honouring the dignity innate within every person? In fact are they not interchangeable?' In this regard, Dr Oppenheimer writes:

> May I suggest that dignity is an endowment of persons themselves in their own right; whereas 'respect' is one way of indicating what we owe to them when we acknowledge their proper dignity. As you rightly say, to offer respect is to recognise and indeed facilitate people's own dignity. What makes this important as a matter of ethics is that so often people's rightful dignity is so concealed as to be hard to find. Especially when people are ill, so many symptoms and so many treatments are deeply undignified, and as a patient one may find this even more unbearable than discomfort and painfulness. So it is a particularly important nursing skill, sometimes more important than gentleness, to be able to treat people in such a way as to make them feel that *dignity still belongs to them* [emphasis mine]. There is a line of

T.S. Eliot in *The Cocktail Party*, 'reluctance of the body to become a thing' (Oppenheimer, *Making Good*, p. 175)

The recognition of the dignity of the other person is first stimulated by the awareness and acceptance of the sacredness of my own dignity. As wounds speak to wounds, could it not be that dignity speaks to dignity, in a way that is affirming of others? There is today a sense of a loss of dignity among those who feel outside the norms of society; especially elderly people who feel that for various reasons they are 'past it, why bother?' An elderly person does not lose their dignity. More often than not, it is the rest of humanity who deny older people the dignity of who they are and were before the physical, mental, social and spiritual changes normal to the ageing processes set in. Clearly the least we can do for older people – and all others who feel left out – is to show them the respect and dignity they undeniably deserve, thereby affirming to them the fact that they really are an integral part of society. This also includes the dying, who need to be assured that they are *living* in their dying.

I am reminded of this whenever I think of or reread the story of Joseph Carey Merrick, a man with horrible physical deformities that were almost impossible to describe, with a head so large that if he lay down he would break his neck. He was known as the 'Elephant Man', imprisoned and cruelly treated by a Victorian circus sideshow manager who tormented him unmercifully. Hounded, persecuted and starving, Merrick ended up one day outside Liverpool Street station where he was rescued by Frederick Treves, a distinguished surgeon who took him in, fed him and cared for him. To Treves' surprise, he discovered during the course of their friendship that lurking beneath the mass of Merrick's corrupting flesh lived a spirit as courageous as it had been tortured, a nature as gentle and dignified as it had been deprived and tormented.

Treves' treatment of Joseph Merrick is an example of compassionate and attentive listening, through and beyond the pain of another's obvious deformities. In the hearing is revealed the soul of a great man, as great as the man who rescued him, and of the others who helped him to know he was human and lovable before he died in the peace of his own small home within the London Hospital. To read the story of the 'Elephant Man' is an inspiration for all who would attempt to hear through listening and be awakened to the fact that within every person, however deformed physically, mentally, socially or spiritually, there is a jewel of human goodness to be constantly polished through the gift of mutual acceptance.

Mattering

Through my work as a listener there comes the realisation that the seeker matters – that we both matter. When Jane comes to see me, I listen to her, thereby showing her that she matters. Through vital activity I am *mattering* Jane. This is the fundamental *raison d'être* for my being involved as a listener.

In my thinking people do matter, and must matter, as persons unique within themselves. This means that what they mind about and what matters to them matters deeply. It is through offering my concerned mattering for the 'other person', through my listening through hearing, that I demonstrate that only he or she matters. For me the most basic right and need for all persons is the right to be listened to and heard non-judgementally. Oppenheimer writes:

> Mattering is a basic concept which is at the heart of any talk about values … it is not to be defined in anything else but we can show what we are talking about by giving examples. Each one of us has – no, is – an example of what mattering means. I can recognise mattering in my own case and then apply it to others. Each of us can truly say 'I matter' [although, I would suggest, only if I know and accept that I matter]. If you think this sounds selfish, let me refer you to Christ's summary of the law: 'Thou shalt love thy neighbour as *thyself.*' We do love ourselves and that is the standard for everyone else. Christian ethics starts with self-love, it does not end there. (Oppenheimer, 'Mattering', p. 61)

Having worked for several years as a teenager in a nursing home for seniors, I gradually accepted the fact that people, whatever their age or infirmity, mattered in the strongest sense of the word: they mattered in their own right and clearly whatever they brought with them into the nursing home mattered in relation to them. There is no doubt in my mind that it is the mattering of self that nurtures the mattering of others. The pregnant mother, to the extent that she is self-mattering, will be able to be mattering of the evolving birth within. This is where, hopefully, for most of us a sense of being mattered or not will affect our future once born. Oppenheimer writes:

> The principle that *people matter* is, I believe a great improvement upon respect for persons [I sense it is in this respect that we recognise the mattering needs of the other person.] ... If we like, we can translate 'mattering' more grandly into 'sacredness' of persons; but I think that 'mattering' though more informal, is also less legalistic and potentially more comprehensive than sacredness.
>
> (ibid., p. 63)

It is my belief that when we say that people matter we are including all those who are rejected either by themselves or through society's greed, through any form of fanaticism whether political or religious, or through the various sources of fear in the lives of many persons – the fear that blinds us to the fact that individuals do matter, whatever the source of their falling short of the mark. As listeners it is very important to accept the fact that the most unattractive and seemingly quite unlovable persons do indeed matter and are so often looking for the person who will affirm to them that they matter, thereby in time enabling them to matter to themselves. Thankfully those who are not being mattered by self or others *are* being mattered by God, who cannot and will not be 'non-mattering' or 'non-accepting'. As Tschudin writes:

> What we do as people cannot ever adequately be described; sooner or later we reach an end with words and concepts and love is the only means of describing that which we do to others. ... I believe that what Oppenheimer is trying to express is what many before her have been trying to express eloquently, and what every nurse tries to express. And what every nurse tries to express, more or less eloquently, and certainly practically, is the search for what makes us human; what it means to be human; and how this is expressed.

Trying to answer this will lead us to others as well as away from them. We are attracted as well as revolted by others. We are ourselves attracted to some and revolting to others. When all is said and done, many of us will say with St Augustine 'Love, and do what you will'. What matters is that we are not afraid of loving, whatever 'loving' means.'

(Tschudin, V., p. 80)

One of the main springboards of hearing through listening is mattering and being mattered. How marvellous that people are so uniquely different to be cherished and mattered. Clearly people do matter. 'People matter; mattering matters; and mattering is more given than chosen' (Oppenheimer, 'Mattering', p. 60). Through our growing awareness of this fact, we are assisting in opening up the space of awareness where people are empowered to matter to themselves and be freed to be mattering of others (ibid., p. 67).

Mattering, like listening and hearing at its best, is being co-mattering, essential for a life worth living and dying for as we continue our journey through the evolving mysteries of our lives.

Simply Being There

Betty had seen me on television a couple of weeks before she made her phone call, asking if I would see her. I agreed. She arrived, very hesitant on entering my flat, and sat tentatively on the edge of the chair, staring at me with her piercing eyes: she was very dishevelled, badly dressed and her body odour suggested she had not had a bath for a long time. During the whole of her visit, all Betty said, or rather asked, was 'Are you real?' She then walked out without saying another word.

I had heard no more from Betty for about a month when one day she suddenly appeared at my door, still dishevelled but not so anxious. This time she made herself at home and accepted a cup of coffee. Gradually she began to talk about not caring for herself, about her personal untidiness and that of her flat, and how she had not been able to work for three years. She also spoke about her inability to get on with her mother. On a subsequent visit she announced that she had cleaned her bathroom, had taken a bath and washed her hair. Our meetings were never very vocal; they were more like a Quaker Meeting. On a further occasion Betty told me she had written to her mother after a lapse of many years. Clearly something was going on within her inner depths. Through our years of simply and quietly being there together, changes started occurring for her.

I remember our last meeting as well as I remember our first. Betty arrived having just come from her hairdresser, smartly dressed and with the news that she had found work as a private secretary. Through having the courage to face and respond to the truth of her potential for change, Betty had begun to matter to herself. I hope that through the attentiveness of my listening, Betty was gradually learning herself how to listen and hear the meaning of her own story.

In asking me 'Are you real?', Betty was asking 'Am I real?' I believe it is crucial for those involved in the process of counselling not to forget that often the answer lies in the seeker's question.

Love overcomes fear

All that I have to offer in this ministry of hearing through listening comes from the strengths of my own weaknesses, my own need for healing, and my own hidden gifts. The addiction of fear will only be released with love's hope of embracing fear; through love's vulnerability to fear and in the awareness that fear creates labels and that love creates persons. My own greatest fear was, and still is to a lesser degree, nurtured by fears of rejection by family and friends; fear of being refused promotion; fear of being physically, socially, sexually and spiritually abused through the Church's condemnation of my sexual orientation; fear of my partner being affected and hurt because of our evolving love for each other.

The first priest to whom I dared to speak about my sexuality had been recommended to me. Yet he responded to me with, 'You are a pervert, you are beyond God's love and you will go to hell if you continue in your depraved activities.' I left his office crying, feeling utterly abused and beaten, mentally and spiritually. And I am not alone. Hundreds of men and women have experienced similar negative responses.

A few years later I felt I should offer the same information about my sexuality to my trustees, even though I feared being told 'We are no longer able to support you.' Instead they embraced me, saying, 'Are we not all brothers and sisters of each other within the Christian faith and the community of all God's people?' and inviting me to eat with them. I at once felt affirmed, and recalled St Paul's words – 'the truth shall make you free.'

Since being ordained, I have made a point of informing successive bishops that I am a non-heterosexual person, i.e. that I am gay. I have found no rejection. To be able to live and be the truth of my natural birthright has released me from living an untruth, or rather the truth that everyone knows but which 'we don't speak about', an attitude forced upon all clergy by the Church's theological stance. I marvel at the gifts of the co-creative and co-healing potential of people's differing sexualities, which are part of the richness and dignity of the differences throughout the whole of God's creation.

The telling of my own story is very important, and has become even more so at an age when I am beginning to live and share the generous fruits of my senior years. Being listened to and heard throughout my life by 'soul friends' and others has been very affirming. Confirming the very real fact that I matter, this encourages me to matter to myself, that I might all the more be mattering of others.

The church's ruling that homosexual and lesbian priests or religious should live a celibate life is, I believe, unrealistic. Moreover, I know that unless one grows naturally towards the gift of celibacy, it will not become a reality whatever one's gender or sexual orientation. No one has the power to enforce celibacy. It is a gift from God. It is manifested from within, and with the support and understanding of others, in the awareness it is a gift, similar to that of our differing sexualities and genders. There is no doubt that a fully 'inspirited body' need no longer be organised, imprisoned through our fears and defence mechanisms; rather we would be unafraid of being vulnerable, erotic, embraced as we are by a spirituality connected to the symphony of love for self, others and all creation.

5

Journeying through self-listening

*Listening is the aspect of
silence in which we
receive the commission
of God.*

*Listening is indeed vital,
but we must take care
to remember that to
understand is to
stand under the other.*

*When one really loves
words become less important
and listening brings deeper
awareness and greater sensitivity of love.*

Mother Mary Clare, SLG

I am now about to share my autobiography. This sharing is essential if I am to understand my story, my journey, so that I may be freed to listen and hear the other person's story. Every story is unique to the person who has the courage of hope to share it with others.

I was born in Canada, in Calgary, Alberta, in June 1927. When young I had a very negative view of myself, fed by comments such as 'You will never amount to much', 'You will never go far', 'You are not very bright'. I never felt I belonged or that I was truly a member of my family. Only years later did I begin to understand why, when what I had always suspected was confirmed: I had been born out of wedlock and, as a result, had been placed in a private orphanage in Vancouver, BC within two or three months of my birth and then forgotten until I went to live with my foster family.

My confidence as a teenager was very low. My sense of being looked after was clear; my awareness of being loved much less so. This sense of insecurity, I suspect, was further enhanced through being a rather shy and dutiful son well into my teens. I needed to be seen as a 'good boy' – 'What would we do without him?' My severe lack of confidence increased as I became sexually aware of myself, and found that I was drawn to other teenage boys. As was the norm in my generation, any discussion of the gift of sexuality, and especially of homosexuality, was simply not on. There was no way in which I could speak with other members of the family about my feelings and desires. I was brought up in a very Victorian manner. Children were 'to be seen and not heard', or as it was put another way, 'Little pigs have very big ears' – a saying I so disliked that I would cry whenever I heard it. Now I see this as a compliment. I need a pair of 'big ears', in order to catch all the sounds of words spoken and to hear the meaning of the gaps between words.

My parents owned the Kirkpatrick Nursing Home. Recognised by the provincial government of British Columbia as being a model for all those involved in the care of seniors, its basic philosophy was that 'Nothing is too good for the senior citizens who have given their lives to their communities'. Individual people in a reasonably secure financial position were cared for alongside those receiving health and social benefits; in many instances Peter paid for Paul.

I was fifteen when my father died. If I remember rightly, it was possible to leave school in one's fifteenth year. This was an arrangement of which my mother approved, because she now needed me to help in the home. I did not object; it was good for my young ego to feel needed in this way. I began by cleaning floors, bathrooms and toilets; I worked in the laundry, where all the washing was done by hand in two cement tubs and then hand rolled; I undertook catering services in the scullery, washing dishes and saucepans, keeping kitchen equipment and floor cleaning; I assisted in the preparation and cooking of the food, eventually taking over the catering services. Later I was initiated into the work of caring for the elderly. I made their beds, washed their hands and faces; I shaved and bathed the men; sat with the ill and the dying, and assisted in preparing the bodies of those who had died for viewing by relatives and friends. I had many different jobs and responsibilities.

It was believed, and perhaps rightly, that I would one day become the general manager and possibly the owner of the Kirkpatrick Nursing Home. Therefore it was important that I should be able to do any of the work required by the various staff members – whether it be caring, cooking, general cleaning, general office tasks, or accounts. As a result, I was left with little free time for socialising; in any case this was not encouraged. My mother became ill with cancer when I was eighteen, and I took over the management of the home for six months. It was quite a learning experience.

During 1945 I met Fr Aelred Carlyle, the Roman Catholic chaplain to the home. Before coming to Canada he had been abbot of the monastery at Caldy off the Pembrokeshire coast in Wales. On arriving in British Columbia he had begun working with First Nation people in the interior of the Province. Later, having worn himself out in this ministry, he became chaplain to the BC Penitentiary (which no longer exists), to the Port of Vancouver, and to the nursing home. He lived in the poorest and roughest area of East Vancouver. It was Fr Aelred who first demonstrated to me that every person, including myself, is of real value. He once said to me that he believed God did not know how to reject – that only humans have such a capacity – and that God is our ultimate lover. (I was around seventeen years of age at this time.) He spoke with such conviction that I have never forgotten his words.

As chaplain to the penitentiary, one of Fr Aelred's duties was to escort condemned men to the gallows. He tried to help these men feel they were not all bad, despite what others thought of them or what they thought of themselves. He grieved deeply that he was unable to help any of them recognise their innate core of goodness. He would say, 'This is what they had to offer back to their creator.' Yet, even though he felt he had failed, these thoughts have stayed with me as a basic theme of my life and my care of others. Fr Aelred was my first professional mentor.

Fr Aelred's acceptance of me at that time, his hearing, through attentive listening, of my needs and pain, watered the seedlings of my future. This kind of hearing through listening has become the 'still centre' of an ongoing ministry. I needed, as we all do, to be reminded that what mattered was to be accepted in a non-judgemental way.

During this time signs of restlessness were emerging. Even though I was fearful of doing so, I was beginning to want to break out of my family situation. In fact I made three separate attempts to do just that. First I took a job as an orderly in the Vancouver General Hospital TB ward; then, very briefly, I worked as a galley cook on a ship of the Royal Mail Lines. As I was under twenty-one, in law I was still under parental control and my mother intervened to get me released, because she needed my services in the nursing home. But I made a third attempt to break out, taking a job as a bakery chef in Purdy's Restaurant in Vancouver.

Between each job, however, I returned to the nursing home. I enjoyed caring for the residents. I realise now that, through taking care of the 'elders' (a term my mother preferred to 'patients'), I was able to fulfil my need to prove myself and to be affirmed, and I offer my thanks for the caring I learned from them. Many of the residents had been early pioneers of British Columbia, and I can remember a comment one of them made to me when it became known that I was leaving: 'We will miss you, yet it is right you leave, for your own future as a person.' It was said by a woman who, in the early 1900s, had been secretary to the chief secretary of a president of the United States.

In 1945 I had joined a local music and drama group, and it was there I met a young man named Jim Hall. We 'clicked' at once and quickly grew close to each other. He was the first person who said 'Bill, you're so loveable, so good!' in such a way that I knew it to be true. Within the next couple of years we started sharing a flat, and we went on to share our lives together for the next twenty years, nurtured by our continuing love and support for each other.

Our families and friends saw us as special companions, but in those days it was not done to talk about being in love with one another. We simply got on and quietly lived our lives. During the 1950s we gave each other a gold ring. There was no discussion – on different days each of us simply bought the other a ring, although I never saw our partnership as a marriage. But I always mention, when offering a few words at a wedding, that marriage is the school for developing friendship through the commitment of two people to each other.

When I finally left the nursing home it was for three basic reasons: I had a life that was not to be owned by anyone except myself; Jim and I wished to share our lives and a home; and I was responding to a great desire to go to England to study singing.

It was in the nursing home that I had received my first unofficial training as an auxiliary nurse. Under the direction of a registered nurse and the doctor who attended the residents of the home, I now decided to train as a practical nurse via the Chicago School of Nursing. After two years I qualified as a state enrolled nurse, working for a brief period in the Vancouver General Hospital, and while in Chicago I practised as private nurse to a senior businessman and also occasionally in a black hospital in Harlem. And then we came to England.

Living in London

When we first arrived in England we lived, as so many Canadians did in those days, in Earls Court, in a wet, damp one-room flat in Warwick Road. Little did I know that I would eventually return to the area in 1979 as an ordained priest in the Anglican Church.

During my early years in London I met Allan Campbell, head of the Rosicrucian Order in the United Kingdom, and he was to become a kind of spiritual mentor to me; he and his wife Joan remained lifelong friends even after they moved to Albany in Australia many years ago and I owe a great deal to both of them. Allan Campbell was Director and London Administrator and later became Deputy Grandmaster UK until he moved to Grand Lodge, in San Jose, California. I had been a member of the Rosicrucian Order in Canada and, feeling I should continue the studies offered, it came about that I first visited Watkins Bookshop in Cecil Court, off Charing Cross Road, looking for Rosicrucian books for my studies. There I met Geoffrey Watkins, the son of the shop's founder; he too was to have a considerable influence on my life. I formed a friendship with Geoffrey and his wife Dianna that was to last until their deaths.

Meanwhile, from 1952 to 1955 I was a salesperson in Selfridges (selling pots and pans) and also worked in the music department of Foyle's bookstore. Afterwards, from 1955 to 1957, I was a member of the cabin crew with BOAC (now British Airways), and the opportunity to travel provided me with a tremendous growth-enabling experience. In the early months of 1957, during a stopover in Calcutta, I had literally been shaken out of myself at the sight of such poverty, the hundreds of poor people begging for their very existence outside grand hotels. This was my first experience of poverty in the Third World, and it seemed to be saying to me that my work was to be with those who existed in such places. It dawned on me that I should leave the airline, return to nursing, and offer my services in a poor area, perhaps in Calcutta itself.

Shortly after my return to London I had a pub lunch with Geoffrey Watkins and told him of my experience. He suggested I discuss it with Dr Eric Graham Howe, founder of The Open Way, a kind of 'think tank' for those involved, either as patients or practitioners, in psychiatric and psychotherapeutic clinics. After a discussion with Dr Howe about my experience in Calcutta, I came to the conclusion, considering my background as a registered practical nurse in Canada and Chicago, that I might train for state registration. He pointed out that this might not be a comfortable experience: few men were entering the nursing services (except in the armed forces) at that time, and that those who did were not allowed to join the Royal College of Nurses (RCN).

I was nevertheless determined to go ahead. My nursing training took place at St Charles Hospital in North Kensington, at around the time of the Notting Hill riots (1957–1960), and here I began to recognise that behind the medical and surgical needs of many patients were psychiatric, social and spiritual problems. Having graduated as an SRN in 1960, I was immediately accepted for a postgraduate course in psychiatric nursing with the York Clinic, based at Guy's Hospital in London, where I became the first male postgraduate nurse – quite a new experience both for me and them. While in training I was growing more aware of the spiritual through caring for others, those we labelled 'patients'. As I shared stories with these people in the middle of the night when sleep was difficult, shared their beliefs, non-beliefs and fears, I was developing a growing sense of the innerness of the other person. During this period I remember having several discussions with Max Saint, chaplain to Guy's, which were to have a profound effect on my future. As a student nurse at St Charles I had experienced the poverty of those living in the poorer parts of Notting Hill Gate; after completing my training, rather than return to Calcutta I decided to stay on in London.

The wounded healer

Following my postgraduate course I assisted in setting up St Luke's, an emergency psychiatric unit at the Middlesex Hospital near Archway in North London for people who, whatever label they had been given, needed to feel they were in a safe place and an accepting environment. During a team consultancy one day a patient named Mary, who displayed psychotic tendencies and who had seemed to be paying no attention to the proceedings, suddenly looked at me and asked, 'Why are you a homosexual?' I was shattered. As far as I was aware, this was not one of my obvious features, but through that brief question my vulnerability was exposed to all by another, equally vulnerable person. It was through Mary that I began to understand that wounds speak to wounds, as they have nothing to hide. Her insight clearly proved to me that we are all called to be 'wounded healers'.

Soon after this experience, in 1972, I discovered a new book by Henri Nouwen, a Roman Catholic priest, called *The Wounded Healer*. Since then Nouwen's name, his ministry and his life have become synonymous with that phrase. Through his personal wounds and his writing he has inspired many, including myself, within the various fields of care. Michael Ford in his biography of Nouwen, *Wounded Prophet*, reminds us that he did not, however, invent the concept, but came across it during his psychological training and later popularised it. It was Carl Jung, in the autobiographical *Memories, Dreams, Reflections*, published in the 1960s, who had written: 'the doctor is effective only when he himself is affected. Only the wounded physician heals' (p. 44). Henri Nouwen would say that his own wounds were to prove that this is as true of the priest as the physician. He explains that

Christ had given this story a fuller interpretation and significance by making his own broken body the means to liberation and new life. Likewise, ministers who proclaim liberation were not only called to care for other people's wounds but to make their own wounds into an important source of healing. They were called to be wounded healers. The wounds he often spoke of were those of alienation, separation, isolation, and loneliness – ones he shared himself (Ford, *Wounded Prophet*, p. 45)

I believe it is also through the mutuality of listening between the seeker and the listener that we both become wounded healers. This is clearly spelled out in one of Nouwen's last books, *Adam: God's Beloved*, in which he describes his journey with Adam, a profoundly disabled young man, whom he cared for at Daybreak. He found the role of carer extremely challenging but ultimately rewarding, and tells in the book of what he learned from Adam. After Adam's death he wrote:

Here is a man who, more than anyone else, connected me with my inner self, my community, and my God. Here is a man I was asked to care for, but who took me into his life and into his heart in such an incredibly deep way. Yes, I had cared for him during my first year at Daybreak and had come to love him so much, but he has been such an invaluable gift to me. Here is my counsellor, my teacher, and my guide, professor, or spiritual director.

He describes Adam as 'the most vulnerable person I have ever known and at the same time the most powerful'. It is an incredible story of two men who through their differing wounds become co-healers one of the other.

Learning to Listen
Through the RCN I now met Barbara Robb, founder of the pressure group AEIGIS (Action Group on the Care of the Elderly in Mental Hospitals). I had been asked to visit her with the aim of stopping her from publishing material on the inadequate care of the elderly in psychiatric hospitals at that time. 'Think of the

harm it would do to nurses!' Unlike myself, however, Barbara was open-minded. We heard each other out and, having listened and understood, I agreed to join her group. Her research was so thorough that I could do nothing else. 'Think of the harm it would do to patients if I did not sign!' Her book, *Sans Everything – A Case to Answer* was published in 1967, and it created quite a stir.

My involvement with Barbara through AEIGIS caused me to pose a question to myself: Why did young nurses, entering the service through their own choice, full of concern for the ill and wounded, within a few years find it quite easy to be so uncaring towards their patients? My initial meeting with Barbara had taught me that we may not hear the other person if either comes to the meeting with preconceived or fixed ideas. ('How dare this woman accuse nurses of being uncaring?') My in-depth involvement with AEIGIS clearly demonstrated that participants in such pressure groups are encouraged to be vulnerable to the truth of knowing they matter and that they have something to say.

There is no doubt that institutions can and do inhibit staff from becoming involved in investigative internal situations for a variety of reasons, often the fear of reprisals from management or others. My association with Barbara, the 'fearless champion' of the elderly in mental hospitals, was not appreciated. Although she experienced far greater animosity than I did, my own involvement hardly endeared me to the nursing community.

Then, in 1967, I was offered the post of charge nurse to assist in developing one of the first drug dependency units in the UK, at St Clement's Hospital in Bow – part of the Royal London Hospital in the East End. It soon became quite clear to me that if we were to empower chemical abusers to let go of their addiction, a great deal of mutual listening would be needed. This could only begin if each person was accepted non-judgementally, affirmed as individuals who mattered to the team and, more importantly, to themselves as persons. The continuing task of the care team was to listen in such a manner that we could hear the pain of others and be vulnerable towards their goodness and uniqueness, which was so easily overshadowed by the ravages of chemical abuse or the stigma of the label 'chemical abuser'.

Early on, it became quite clear that nurses working in the unit needed to spend time in the community, visiting patients in their homes. This was essential for proper assessment of the real situation, so as to be able to see where further help might be needed, and for developing an awareness of the factors that might help the care team to assist and encourage the patient in letting go of their drugs of choice. Through this shared listening the community care team was established, and a new nursing position was eventually developed, the Community Psychiatric Nurse (CPN).

During 1969 I left St Clement's and the London Hospital for the post of Assistant Regional Nursing Officer with the North West Regional Hospital Board in London, with specific responsibility for psychiatric, mentally and physically impaired patients as well as for nursing personnel. It was through the Regional Board that the training and development of the Community Psychiatric Nursing programme was initiated at Chiswick College, West London. Today, 35 years on, CPNs are a vital part of overall nursing and other care disciplines in the community.

Other improvements followed. Again at the Board's request, and in conjunction with The King's Hospital Fund, we set up a two-year programme under Professor R. Evans to examine why there was a need for a change in nursing attitudes. What emerged was a sense that patients were not being accepted as people. This was borne out by the prevalence of certain undignified practices, such as bathing several patients in the same bath water and without screens around them, combined with an 'Oh well, it has to be done, let's get it over with' attitude. Such practices denied the dignity of the patient as a person, something we recognised to be detrimental to both the patient and the nurse. In such situations the patient becomes a disease with a number, ceasing to be seen as a person and no longer being afforded the respect that is their natural birthright – especially when the patient is elderly, or vulnerable in any way.

Such an attitude may be due to the fact that there appears to be no satisfaction in nursing those who are chronically or mentally impaired. It is difficult in such situations for many nurses to take time to break down the 'them and us' situation. Yet I learned to be grateful for such patients. They were the first I was privileged to care for. They taught me how to be alongside them in their lostness, their uniqueness. Whenever the sacred gift of listening was offered it helped patients to feel they mattered.

During 1971 I resigned from the Regional Board. By now I was growing aware that my best contribution to the services was to be able to offer person-to-person care, working with small groups, but I also made the decision because I am not an institutional person: I would rather be on the edge yet in the centre. As a result, I left the Board and the statutory services for the voluntary care sector. Being a board officer had nevertheless provided another steep learning curve in my life, an experience that I felt privileged to share.

Centrepoint

Within weeks of leaving the Board, George Ellison, then Bishop of London, aware of my previous involvement in the East End, asked me to succeed Fr Ken Leech, the radical founder of Centrepoint in Soho. This was a project located in the basement of St Anne's House, providing temporary overnight shelter and assistance, food and advice, for young people new to London who found themselves homeless and at risk. I was appointed chair of the management committee and within six months became the full time co-ordinator of the project.

Our volunteers prepared the centre each evening to receive the young people waiting outside the gate on Shaftesbury Avenue. On admittance, after a few basic questions had been asked, they were provided with social and sleeping areas, shower and toilet facilities, and a substantial evening meal and breakfast before leaving the next morning. It was a place where they were able to discuss their immediate needs and where they could be given advice and introduction to other projects, such as the Soho Day Centre Project, founded and run by Lil Butler. Assistance with arranging further accommodation could be offered, or help provided in finding work or a return home if that was their wish. Some, of course, did not want to return home.

James was just seventeen when he arrived in London from a

small town in the Midlands. The few pounds he had brought with him had dwindled to a few pence by the time he reached Centrepoint. He had already spent two days and a night walking the streets. The first two people who offered him help had been out to exploit him; the third had directed him to Centrepoint. James had a lucky escape. It is no exaggeration to say that hardship and desperation have forced many other young people into prostitution, petty crime and other hidden West End subcultures. Fortunately, after he came to Centrepoint, from where he went on to the Soho Day Centre Project, a hostel place was found for James in South London with young men of his own age, and after registering with the Youth Employment Service he found a job as a junior clerk. Four months after his initial stay in Centrepoint, James revisited both projects, saying that he was happy in his job, was soon due his first holiday and would be going home to spend some time with his family.

As the director of Centrepoint, this was my first venture into the voluntary sector, and I soon became aware that it was quite different from working within the health services. Joining the founding team of radical volunteers, who were in touch with the issues and expected to be involved in all management decisions, I was challenged into a dialogue of decision-making. It was a much more fruitful situation for all concerned, including myself.

Gradually, as attendance in the night shelter grew, so did the volunteer group, now comprising seven volunteers for each night of the week, with about twenty on call at any one time. After a year, I felt that more professional support was needed. A small team of four professionals was established to take on differing aspects of the work. This freed me to concentrate on fundraising, adding to an already busy schedule as director, caring for staff and the volunteer team. I often found myself listening to the stories and needs of the homeless young people as well as the volunteers, each of whom demanded in their own way to be listened to and heard. I was involved with administrative work for the centre, and in forging links with other projects that were making attempts to engage with the needs of homeless young people in central London.

These activities increased my workload, especially the fundraising and administration. Without any real supervision I was working a great deal of overtime, on many occasions trying to manage on six hours' sleep a night. Clearly I was leading the team in their caring of the young people using the night shelter, but I was not caring for myself as I should have been. As a result, one evening on going up to my flat I collapsed, coming to only the next day in the convent of the Sisters of the Love of God (SLG) at Burwash. (I had been taken there as the team knew I used to visit the convent periodically.) I woke to find Sister Elvira looking after me. I was there for about three weeks, of which I spent the whole of the first week in bed; the doctor informed me, 'You are here for two basic reasons, overwork and stress.' During the third week Mother Mary Clare suggested I spend some time convalescing at the convent's Mother House. From our first meeting I felt we had met at a very deep level. It was the beginning of a friendship that ended only when she died.

Then, during the latter part of the same year, I ended up at St Luke's Hospital for Clergy with glandular fever. This time I was away from work for about four weeks.

Both these illnesses were, I suspect, related to the fact that I was not paying full attention to my various needs. They may also have been linked to major changes in my relationship. Even though Jim supported my journey towards the Church, he could not understand why I should want to become involved with an institution that he saw as negative and at odds with the inclusive message of Jesus, especially given its refusal to acknowledge the validity of non-heterosexual relationships such as our own. Nevertheless, as a potential worker-priest, I was moving towards becoming deeply involved with the Christian Movement.

6
My spiritual journey

The spiritual dimension is like a mist which covers our lives from the cradle to the grave

Walter Barbour

My whole life has been a continuing spiritual journey. I was not brought up in a religious family, even though my mother had been a member of the Salvation Army for a short while in her early twenties. However, my sister and I could go to church if we wished, and we did occasionally attend various churches, usually whenever a children's party was being given. To say the least, we were ecumenical Sunday school goers.

Like most teenagers, I let go of the Church because it meant little or nothing to me. However, my sense of wonder, of the mystery and the awesomeness of creation, continued to grow. For me the mystery of God has always been a positive presence. In the early fifties, I started exploring different philosophies and faiths. During this period I became a member of the Rosicrucian Order. A very ancient society supposedly founded in 1484, the Order seeks to synthesise science, philosophy and religion. Rosicrucians believe that all difficulties in life can be made to serve a higher calling if they are borne with patience and humility. The problems we overcome in our life can be instruments of final good, a means to develop our faculties for the good of others. We are purified by suffering on the Cross of Matter in the unfolding of the Rose – the symbol of the Soul. We seek to become a friend to the neglected, a guard for those in mortal danger, an encouragement to the weak; we aim to engender self-respect in the erring, give knowledge to the ignorant and inward joy to the sorrowing. And in so doing we give contentment and hope to ourselves.

It was through the teaching of the Rosicrucians that I was

introduced to various thinkers and rituals. The latter spoke to me of the mystery in ways that words did not. By hearing through listening to the mystery within the ritual, I had embarked on an inner journey that was to continue throughout my life.

I have already mentioned how, in 1953, while I was engaged in a search for books recommended for the Order's various study courses, I was introduced through Allan Campbell to Geoffrey Watkins, son of the founder of Watkins Books. It was during one of my many visits to the bookshop that Geoffrey began recommending to me books he thought especially relevant to my studies. He would suggest the desert fathers and mothers, the mystics – in particular Julian of Norwich, St Teresa of Avila, St John of The Cross, St Aelred of Rievaulx, as well as such books as *The Way of The Pilgrim* and *The Cloud of Unknowing*. I mentioned to Geoffrey that I was interested in becoming a Buddhist. His reply was, 'Few westerners become Buddhists; however, such study would enrich your Christian studies.' He gave me a copy of Meister Eckhart's *Sermons*, suggesting I read them slowly.

As I have also mentioned, it was Geoffrey who introduced me to Dr Eric Graham Howe, a Christian-Buddhist and founder of The Open Way. He was a pioneer, in the manner of Carl Gustav Jung, in reconciling the wisdom of East and West and, like James Hillman, was deeply interested in restoring the 'soul' to its psychological sense. The Open Way held weekly meetings linking different views of the wholeness of life through the insights of psychology, philosophy and the various faiths. These meetings, either led by Dr Howe or chaired by him when there was a guest speaker, lasted for about one and half hours. I would often attend, though I had difficulty in understanding their content. Dr Howe was the author of many books. One that particularly affected me was itself titled *The Open Way*, and its theme was acceptance. There is no doubt in my mind that both Geoffrey and Eric, like Allan Campbell, were my 'soul friends' until their deaths.

During the late fifties I met James Cairn-Cross, an actor, at a social gathering. We had a long conversation about religion. James was a committed Roman Catholic, while at the time I thought of myself as an agnostic, although not anti-Christian.

The next day I received through the post a copy of a book that caused me to think seriously about the 'Christian Way'. It was Simone Weil's *Waiting on God*. I was struck by her honesty, and thought of her too as a Christian agnostic. On my first reading I was impressed by the whole book, but there were a few sentences that really spoke to me. It also introduced me to Revd Fr Perrin – one of the founders of the Worker Priest Movement in France.

Taizé and Beyond

During my training as an SRN I had an experience that had to be listened to and heard before I could begin to understand its meaning. Like all 'peak experiences' it is difficult to explain. All I am really sure of is the fact that I was completely lifted out of myself. How do you explain a sunrise or sunset that has you gazing in wonder, or the power of music, the effect of a field full of red poppies or rich in the yellow of large sunflowers, or the feeling when your team has scored and won the match?

The experience occurred while I was taking in an exhibition of Salvador Dali's artistic jewellery in a Bond Street jewellery shop. I was particularly struck by the most ambitious of all the jewels, the 'Angel Cross'. In Dali's words this represents 'The treatise of existence to existence – the gradual transformation from the mineral world to the angel.' This creation incorporates three crosses. One is sculpted of gold; the second, of coral, represents the Tree of Life; the third is the overall frame, composed of five cubes of 18-karat gold. The whole rests upon a lapis lazuli globe and rises above the sulphate base and the moving diamond and platinum spines. The crucifix is not a literal representation of Christ, for the face and figure are not depicted as he was known on earth. As designed and painted by Dali, the figure represents 'the angelic state achieved by man when he detaches himself completely from material surroundings'.

As I stood there I was transfixed by a cluster of dark red rubies created in the shape of a heart alongside the Angel Cross. They appeared to be pulsating like a regular heart beat, as though the piece was beating along with my own heart. The combination of the Angel Cross and the pulsating ruby heart caused me to stand transfixed, for how long I do not know. Strangely I do not remember arriving home.

The next thing I was aware of was lying on my bed for a rest prior to going on night duty at the hospital. The whole room appeared to have changed completely, to be bathed in the golden warmth of love, the love of total acceptance. I sensed I had been touched, embraced by something delicately wonderful, and yet fearful in that I could understand its meaning for me.

I was quite surprised when, after many years, I again looked at the pictures of the exhibition in the catalogue and saw that the appearance of the Angel Cross was not quite the same as I remembered seeing it. Perhaps I had been seeing at a deeper level. Who knows? But what was missing entirely from the photo was the cluster of dark red rubies created in the shape of a heart.

At any rate, it was as a result of this experience during the late 1950s that I contacted Taizé, a Protestant community near Cluny in France. I had seen an article about the community in *Time* magazine and I immediately felt I should go there, so I telephoned and asked if I could come for a retreat, my first ever. The guest master, Brother Laurent, was very welcoming, as were all the brothers. I felt I could be a part of the community, living as they do a simple life and not being given to religious fundamentalism.

Brother Laurent and I had daily meetings; he listened, and I felt he heard. With his guidance, I wrote out the first confession of my life. I met him one morning in the community's private chapel in the little village church, and handed it to him. He simply laid it on the altar to be accepted by God. He then gave me absolution and returned the script to me, saying I should burn it as it was between God and myself. I was so impressed by the service that I have never forgotten it. It taught me how valuable it was to have offered and been forgiven through the ultimate forgiveness of God.

On the evening before my departure Brother Laurent and I had a long discussion, during which I asked about the possibility of testing my vocation to the religious life within the community. He made no immediate answer except to say he would talk with Brother Roger, the Prior, and that I should have lunch with them both the next day. We shared a simple meal, followed by a discussion as to the testing of my vocation (if in fact I had one) with a view to my eventually being professed to the community. We all agreed that my desire was tinged with emotionalism – not a sound basis for such a major change of life, nearing the age of forty as I was. It was suggested, however, that if I felt as strongly in five years then they would reconsider.

Three years later I was invited back. It was January, and there were very few guests around. On my last day I met both Brothers Roger and Laurent while walking towards the Prior's house, and we spoke as with one voice. While I cannot remember the exact words, they were to the effect that a life within their community was not for me and that another way would show itself in the future. I felt this to be right. Indeed I had said to myself on waking that morning, 'This way is not to be the way for me at this time.'

Within eighteen months of my last visit to Taizé, I had another experience on what was to have been a two-week holiday in Ajaccio in Sardinia. Having been informed by the tourist agency in London that there was no need to make reservations, when I arrived I found that there was 'no room in the inn'. I was eventually directed to a fisherman's cottage and put up in the family bed; as my hosts told me, 'You are too tall for the guest bed.' The bedroom contained many pictures and statues, although they could not be seen when I lay in bed. During the night I was awakened by the presence at the end of my bed of the most beautiful woman I had ever seen. Saying nothing, she reached out with her outstretched arms without actually touching me.

When I showed an early draft of the manuscript of this book to a friend, a former priest and religious, he commented about my Sardinian experience that 'This is about Mother or Love's energy and Mother Bill.' And at the same time he informed me that 'Gandhi referred to himself as mother.' The immediate question I asked myself was, 'Was this Mother Bill reaching out to Father Bill?' Then I remembered that St Francis used to refer to the head of each house within his community as the Guardian Mother. I asked myself, was this a reference to the fact that both male and female energies can be found in each person embraced by the Father and Mother love of God?

As a result of my experience in Sardinia I flew home the next day and spoke to Geoffrey Watkins about it. He suggested that I have a talk with Dr Howe, who in turn suggested I see a priest. I disagreed; I felt I should be seeing a psychiatrist. We finally agreed that I would see both. The psychiatrist thought I might have had a slight schizophrenic experience but that I should not worry.

I finally met with the Revd Joseph McCulloch of St Mary-le-Bow, Cheapside in the City of London. It is difficult to remember our discussions in detail; however, I remember the general themes. In our early sessions he spent most of the time 'being there' – listening, and thereby allowing me to start wherever I chose. At first I talked about my families, both my biological family and my adopted family in Vancouver. I shared stories of my early life in the nursing home, my education, my eventual involvement in the home and my various reasons for leaving. The last four weeks were more structured: I talked about my ideas on religion, my interest in Christianity, Buddhism and interfaith generally; the Rosicrucian Order, my various spiritual experiences in London, Sardinia and southern France, my reasons for going to Taizé and eventually about my first confession with Brother Laurent and how it had impressed me.

The final two meetings were devoted to discussions relating to the Christian faith, especially around baptism, confirmation and the Christian way of life. And, towards the end of our last meeting, I asked to be baptised. The sacrament was performed in the chapel of the Holy Spirit in St Mary-le-Bow in May 1958, and I was confirmed in the Commonwealth Chapel in St Paul's Cathedral later in May 1958.

Journeying towards Christ

In the early sixties, while I was involved in postgraduate training as a psychiatric nurse in the York Clinic at Guy's Hospital and Holloway Sanatorium, I would often have discussions with Max Saint, the hospital chaplain. I would question why many patients returned and whether it had anything to do with not being committed or nurtured by a faith. I remember one woman saying to me, 'I've been baptised and confirmed but it's done nothing for me, it has no meaning for me.' It was during this period that Mary, a patient suffering severe depression, gave me a small book, first published in 1910 and still being reprinted, entitled *Christ In You*. As I glanced through the book, the first words that stood out in my memory were 'Heaven is not a place, but a consciousness of God.'

About three months later the chaplain suggested I meet a friend of his, Canon Sidney Evans. As I later found out, Evans was the first principal of the Southwark Ordination Course for men (it is now open to women as well) who wished to be ordained while remaining in their area of work as worker priests, a presence of Jesus in their midst. We had a very long discussion and finally he asked me what I thought of adopting such a role. I believe I said something like, 'Very interesting. Well, yes,' assuming that all newly confirmed priests would attend classes on how to be and live the Christian way of life. A few days later I met with Canon Frank Colquhoun, the assistant director of the course. Eventually a letter arrived from him stating the dates of the course and within a month I was enrolled, even then not really understanding what I had agreed to.

The course was to last for three years, and as it was the first of its kind a 100 per cent pass was required at the end of the final year. My test papers in the second year indicated that I might not make the grade. It was then suggested that I join a theological college for a further two years. The Revd Harold Wilson, Head of Salisbury Theological College, agreed to my becoming a student and to my being ordained as a nurse worker-priest. I spent the next two years at the college, leaving in 1966. After some delay, I was ordained deacon in St Mary's Bow in the East End of London on Ascension Day 1968 by the then Bishop of Stepney, Everard Lunt; in fact I was the last person he was to ordain before his retirement. At the end of the service Bishop Lunt said that it was one of the best ordinations he had been involved with – 'How wonderful, everyone seemed to know you.' A great reception at the Royal London Hospital followed.

In 1970 Bishop Trevor Huddleston arrived as the new Bishop of Stepney. We had a lengthy discussion, at the end of which he said he would ordain me a priest on St Michael and All Saints Day, 29 September 1970, in St Mary's Parish Church, Islington.

Having now been fully ordained, I spent three years as a nurse worker-priest, and was then licensed to St Mary-le-Bow (1970),

St Anne's, Soho (1971) and St Cuthbert's in Earls Court (1979). Most of my ministry has been with people who for a variety of reasons found themselves on the fringes of society. In the early seventies, by which time I was deeply involved in the Centre-point project, I became a priest associate of the Sisters of the Love of God at their Mother House in Oxford. At this time I had many conversations with Mother Mary Clare and the idea of taking up a religious life resurfaced. In fact, after leaving Centrepoint in 1975 I spent three months in the SLG commu-nity. As a result, I felt I could do nothing but test my vocation within the Anglican Society of St Francis.

Prior to doing so, however, I spent a wonderful, carefree month with the Roman Catholic Franciscans in the small monastery of San Damiano in Assisi. It was during the last two weeks of my stay that I met Brother Raymond SSF, who was joining the novitiate at the same time as myself. Raymond's charismatic enthusiasm was infectious. We laughed, sang, ran up and down the hills, and spent much time in prayer in the various chapels within the cathedral and elsewhere in the area. When we parted Raymond went to the Friary at Alnmouth in Northumberland. On being fully professed he became Brother Ramon, staying in the community, enriching it and many others beyond the community itself. For many years he lived, initially outside the enclosure, as a community hermit. Alongside his work as a 'soul friend' to many, Brother Ramon became popular as a writer on prayer and the religious life. It is one of my great regrets that we did not keep in touch.

In the community I became Br Aelred William; I chose the name Aelred thinking of Fr Aelred Carlyle and St Aelred of Rievaulx, who both understood what love was about. During my period with the community I was a member of various mission teams, both to local parishes and to the community's own school at Hook. We visited Broadmoor psychiatric hospital one Holy Week; later I spent a month in a small skete with Brother Harold at Alnwick, Northumberland. This was followed by a year in the community's enclosure at Glasshampton, in Worcestershire.

At that time Br Alban, the Guardian, was able to offer much helpful discernment; and these last two postings were an indi-cation for me that I was growing towards a deeper type of self-listening, that the mystery of myself was causing me to question whether I might be moving towards a spiritual, perhaps a more contemplative, way of life. But where? I asked Brother Alban. He said, 'Brother, relax! Let our blessed Francis of Assisi, or St Aelred of Rievaulx, be your guide. Let yourself go into the Cloud of Unknowing.'

On leaving the Society of St Francis in the latter part of 1978 I went to live for three months as a solitary in the small village of Rushton, near Accrington in Lancashire. It was a time for reflecting on what my future might be. I now felt I was being prepared for the work of being a contemplative activator, but where? Eventually I came to Earls Court, on the western edge of Central London.

Today, thirty years later, I suggest that anyone who attempts to live his or her life to the full is living a spiritual (rather than a religious) life. Such a life, I believe, can be lived almost anywhere, if nurtured by prayer and the sacraments. I believe there is a continuing call for differing kinds of ecumenical and interfaith cells of co-creativeness.

Part 2

Responding

The Mystery of Love
May I be still enough to hear, in the beating of my heart, Love's echo, the Love that made the stars, that made me. And may that Love reverberate in my heart too, so that I may truly hear and reach out to all whom I meet. May I be there for them, for Love. Amen.

Anonymous

7

My journey through love's endeavouring

> How often have we really been heard in our lives? To be wholly listened to is one of the greatest of affirmations we can receive. It is rare; it is to be recognised, remembered, reminded that we have a value, a right to be alive – not for what we do, for what we have done or are going to do, but for who we are, becoming the person that we ourselves may have never heard.
>
> Roger Housden

> For what the ear hears, the mind forgets. What the heart hears, time can never erase.
>
> Matthew the Poor

I may only respond to the ministry of hearing through listening by recognising the strengths of my own weaknesses. I am given to this area of concern from within my own personal life experiences, from a growing awareness and acceptance of myself as a person. I know that I can do no other but simply be God's minister of love and hope, to be shared with the wounded, in any place and situation, according to the needs of each person. I am called to be *simply a presence*, as best I am able, and to be a sign of the divine love of God, in the sure knowledge of faith, the certainty that no person is beyond the love and hope of God. My desire is simply to be a very human icon of Jesus our Brother of love; of Mary our Mother of love, within the Father's all-embracing love, in the belief that we are all born to be lovers. Love is our calling. To be loved and to love is our basic calling.

I continue to be enriched and guided into this ministry of love and hope by people from every walk of life, especially by the elderly and the young, through their visible and invisible wounds. I have the privilege of embracing them, offering them love and hope in the awareness that this is a mutual activity between the listener and the seeker. Within these attempts I have often found myself not being fully the lover a Christian is called to be through baptism. Yet all have gifted me with the spirit of care-fullness for the growth of the person, that her soul will be encouraged; an agonising and joyful responsibility shared with each other and our creator, as we continue to evolve body and soul towards our fullest potential. Simone Weil writes:

> I have the essential need, and I think I can say vocation, to move among men of every class and complexion, mixing with them and sharing their life and outlook, so far that is to say as conscience allows, merging into the crowd and dis-appearing among them, so that they show themselves as they are, putting off all disguises with me. It is because I long to know them so as to love them just as they are. For if I do not love them as they are, it will not be they whom I love, and my love will be unreal.
>
> (Weil, *Waiting on God*, p. 48)

I have a growing awareness that truth will release me into being a person of truth towards others. Hopefully it will allow me to clarify, for myself and for others, the ministry of love we need to share and receive from each other. In the final analysis, I give myself within the ongoing ministry of God the lover for a whole variety of reasons. I need to be needed; to feel useful; to love and be loved; to grow with and through those who come into the orbit of my immediate concern; to be and to share with those persons who are often wounded through their families. I have increasingly come to know that it is the wounds of our fathers and mothers, rather than their sins, that are passed on to other members of the family. I am also in this ministry to share with those who exist within the various secular and non-secular insti-tutions that tend to depersonalise and dehumanise and de-soul the individual.

My empathy, nurtured through compassion, has caused me to covenant myself to the poor of all kinds. For me, having been baptised into the movement of love and hope that is the Church of Christ at its best, this call is *basic*. Love is after all the sole reason for the coming into being of the Christian movement: love for *all* God's people, especially the poor of all worlds. Ideally a covenant to the poor is a covenant to being a responsible person towards myself, towards others, towards the all of creation. The basic vocation of every Christian is to accept that there are no outsiders. When Bishop Tutu spoke of the people of South Africa as being 'the rainbow people of God', he reminded us that all the peoples of the world are 'the rainbow peoples of God'. In this light, ours is a call to embrace every soul into a remembrance and acceptance of the very real fact that we are all 'oned' to the soul of our creator, who is our ultimate Mother and Father, whose DNA is carried by all humanity and all of creation. Because of this I feel we should use the vital title of Creator rather than God. This allows us to recognise that God is the Creator in both male and female, as we are all sons and daughters of God.

I write in an attempt to clarify for myself, if for no one else, my own unique life and ministry in relationship to my vocational responsibility to love as a soul-person, as a priest-brother. This is a response to the covenanting of my life to and for the poor, the broken and the lost in our almost non-society, and more especially to the young and the elderly, broken through the addictions of alcohol, drugs and sex, all broken icons of the broken Jesus. The covenant I have made is to share as realistically as possible in their lives, and they in mine, as a lover – as a co-creative rather than as a pro-creative lover. I covenant in the belief that love and hope will lead us towards the healing of the wounds that are the source of so many forms of addiction, because they are linked to fear rather than love, to despair rather than hope.

I believe we are to encourage the wounded to care for each other in recognition of the soul hidden deeply within. The ghettoisation of our wounded sisters and brothers is for me one of the greatest weaknesses of the caring services, both statutory and voluntary. I believe that the wounded are called to serve the wounded, the weak to serve the weak, and the poor to serve the poor. Sister is called to serve sister and brother and brother is called to serve brother and sister, and Christians are called to serve *all* God's peoples.

Like Mary at the foot of the Cross, we are to hold the weak in our laps and in our hearts so closely that they will feel loved, needed, trusted, accepted, forgiven, in such a way that they will be reconciled to themselves, to others and to the mysterious energies of the love force we call God. Yes, I am called to be of service to the poor, especially those made poor by man's inhumanity to man and his inability to see the reality, the soul of the other person. As a Christian I have promised to serve the poor, especially those for whom we have little or no time; those whom the church has labelled sinners and barred from the Love of God, as if that were possible. I believe from deep within my soul that in God there are no sinners, only those who are weak, who have fallen short of the mark according to the Church's criteria. In God, in whom we trust, we are all responsible for the differing gifts of life; to God alone, as creator of our evolving creation, are we accountable.

To have experienced a similar weakness or wounding to that of those I am trying to be alongside is to offer a personal and unique knowledge that may be co-creative and co-healing for all concerned. For me this affirms the fact that there is no 'them and us'. My experience is such as to suggest that for those who are truly open to the Holy Spirit of divine care humanised, our weaknesses do not disturb. Rather they open up new pathways for dialogue, new ways of ministry, of praying, of loving, of offering hope, of sharing in the liberation of others and ourselves: this is the 'good news' of love's unbinding. It is my belief that the truth of our weaknesses and the strengths to be shared will release us into a freedom of being and of growth that is not only wholesome, but also healing for all concerned.

The co-creative love of God

I not only believe, I know that to be gay, i.e. a *non-heterosexual*, is good, healthy, right and normal for me. It is a co-creative gift from God to me, offered co-creatively for myself as well as others. This is true of the whole spectrum of human sexuality when not abused or exploited. As a man who happens to be gay, a Christian and a priest, I am called to be a co-creative, co-healing lover of hope, one who is on the side of human dignity and liberty within a freedom confirmed by and through the gospels of love, hope, justice and peace. These actions are affirmed by the Beatitudes, the Magnificat and the Parables of the New Testament – if you like, the rule book for the Christian. Therefore my commitment, in so far as I am realistically capable of fulfilling it, is to being politically active against all that discriminates, dehumanises, de-souls; all that moralises and is judgemental in the name of legalism rather than love.

I must be against all who see those who are weaker than themselves and those who are wounded, of whatever sexual orientation or gender, as less than persons. I must be against all who see others as sex symbols to be exploited. I must be against all those who are convinced that all homosexuals do is live an orgy of sexual exploitation, either of themselves or others; those whose prejudice never allows them to raise their eyes or minds above the navel of those they are so quick to label as being sick, queer, pervert or worse. I must be against all forms of addiction, including the addiction to exploitation of others through consumerism nurtured by the sense of insecurity, fear and greed.

Many Christians, male and female, eventually fall co-creatively in love with Jesus, who was a healthy man with his own wounds. When we look more closely at our saints and mystics, who are our models and mentors, we soon recognise that their love included love of male for male, love of female for female. Are men only to love women and women only men? Is this not impossible for a Christian, who is called to love irrespective of gender or orientation? In this love, we are fools for love, for Jesus, for our non-gay or gay sisters and brothers. I am called to this ministry of hearing through listening by realising my fullest potential through the strength of my stability of purpose. It is that I may offer the truth of myself and the gift of my imperfections to others, as they offer me theirs: with the great, full acknowledgement that I do nothing of myself but to be myself – Being There.

Reaching Out

While I was living as a kind of hermit in the village of Rushton, I came to London to visit my mentor and friend Geoffrey Watkins, who had retired and was now living in Kensington. On leaving, instead of going to Kensington High Street tube station,

I turned the wrong way and found myself in Earls Court. I had no intention of being in the area, but after wandering around I felt I was being guided to 'be there', and that from now on my primary work would be *to pray and be available* to anyone in the area and beyond. In 1979, Earls Court was one of the poorest areas in London, with the largest population relative to its size in Europe. (Nowadays the area is very different, having become one of the wealthier parts of London.) It was recognised by the EEC as a high priority area where there were many people with mental, social, educational and spiritual problems. They lived in places with few or no cooking or adequate living facilities. Many were fearful of approaching the statutory services, feeling that they would not be given time to be heard and would be treated as second class citizens, when what they were looking for was someone with the time and skill to listen to them, to help them feel that they mattered. Soon after I moved to the area someone remarked to me, 'Your work is to be loitering with intent.'

In order to carry out my listening ministry, I formed with the help of others a small project called 'Reaching Out'. The centre of my ministry was a small chapel under the pavement of Warwick Road. This I had converted out of a coal bunker and dedicated to Mary Magdalene (who was listened to and heard by Jesus, and moved towards a new way of life), and to St Barnabas (who recognised the potential latent within St Paul before the disciples themselves did). The chapel was wrapped in the noise of the constant flow of people walking over it and the sound of onrushing traffic. Here prayers were said daily, and the Eucharist was offered once or twice a week for anyone, including those who came to the centre for help, who wished to share this time with me.

My spiritual models for the centre were the desert fathers and mothers; and in particular Charles de Foucauld. Before his conversion Foucauld was an aristocrat, a soldier and scientist. Following a radical conversion he was called to be a witness to God. He felt drawn to return to the authentic gospel of love and to the acceptance that there are no boundaries between race, culture or religion. He offered his services to the poor and the outcast, his icon being Jesus and his life among the poor and the outcast. He died having been a missionary, a hermit in the Sahara and a mystic. After his death, his vision of service to the poor inspired the foundation of the Little Brothers of Jesus, and later the Little Sisters of Jesus.

It is my belief that the deserts of today are to be found in the inner cities of the world. I believe that in the silences of prayerful attentiveness, all actions of empathy and compassion have a meaning for those who come into the orbit of my concern. I believe that their suffering contains the seeds of healing, to be watered by the energies of love, faith and hope, nurtured by truth and goodness.

Jane, confused, fearful and aggressive towards herself and others, especially the 'professionals who know nothing', one day walked into the café where I was having a meal with my companions. On seeing me she came over and asked, 'Will you hear my confession now?' I suggested to her, as this was a very private matter, that perhaps she would like a blessing instead. I offered the blessing and she went off quite cheerfully with 'Thanks, Father.' I have seen Jane many times since and she has never again asked to have her confession heard.

George, aged seventeen, was out cruising. He met another man with whom he had a few drinks; they met a third man and had a few more drinks. The three went home together, but once there George was gang-raped. I met him in the early hours of the morning, bleeding from the violence committed against his body. I took him to casualty, where I was told he would be having surgery the next day. This brutal attack left him very damaged physically, mentally and spiritually.

Jack saw me in the local bookstore. He asked, 'Are you Father Bill? May I talk with you? I'm in trouble with the police. I've been charged with possession and selling drugs outside the local tube station.' I said 'Yes,' but told him this might not be the best place considering the subject of our discussion. He asked, 'Would you mind coming back to my place? I only live around the corner.' After speaking with him, I became convinced he was not a pusher and rarely touched hard drugs; cannabis was his recreational drug of choice. I wrote a reference for his court appearance, and the magistrate gave him a severe lecture and put him on probation for one year. He left the area and I later heard he was training to become a solicitor.

Listening Across the World

During October 1983 I became involved for the first time with those affected by the challenges of HIV/AIDS; I began to assist many young people to live with their dying, with the varying emotions and needs involved. Most of these young men were homosexual, dying of the pain of being rejected – by a partner, by family members, by work colleagues or others. They wanted to know if God would reject them too. The only answer I could offer was that God does not know how to reject, that he has far more knowledge of the whys and hows of our lives than we can ever know.

I often found myself being an advocate for these young men, for their partners and for members of their families who had difficulty in understanding or accepting the validity of their relationship. On many occasions I was involved in advising on the design of funeral services that would give meaning and validity to the deceased person's life and to those who survived him. These young men taught me much about the mystery and spirituality both of the other person and of God, whom they saw as the greatest of mysteries. They would often refer to God as 'the mystery'.

While I continued this work until 1999, in 1985 I also began increasingly to meet young men involved at street level in the sex industry. It was around the time that a fourteen-year-old boy called Jason Swift was murdered. I was visited by the police; they thought I might have known Jason, but the answer was no. Richie, who had worked with me at Centrepoint, at once said, 'Let's try and set up a centre for young men involved in the sex industry.' My reply was, 'Why not? I'll see if I can find funding.'

At the time it was an innovative and pioneering project. I floated the idea, and was asked to present an outline. And the plan was accepted; we received core funding, with Richie as the co-ordinator, and myself as director and fundraiser, for what became Streetwise Youth, the first organisation of its kind in the UK. Our approach was to offer non-judgemental acceptance and help with the practical problems of homelessness, poor health, financial and legal needs, as well as a place to share with others during the day. Meals were provided; there were showers and clothes-washing facilities, as well as a large kitchen where the young people could be introduced to basic cooking skills. We developed an educational programme around the issues of safer sex and HIV/AIDS, and an outreach programme for making contact with young people involved in prostitution on the streets, in the railway and bus terminals, bars and clubs, offering information on how to reach us and other agencies working with young people alone in central London.

In one of our annual reports, a young man wrote: 'I'm not proud of being a prostitute, but I am proud of being me. That's what Streetwise Youth has taught me. They helped me find my self-respect; they don't judge or criticise, it's a good place to come because you can sit and talk.' Our work was nurtured with the awareness that each person matters, in whatever way he presents himself. We attempted to hear the person hidden within the label and the activity of being a prostitute.

During 1989 there was growing concern that many people throughout Earls Court were still forced merely to exist, rather than live, in shared one-room accommodation in so-called hotels or hostels, with minimal cooking facilities and with no space for socialising. Fr John, the Vicar of St Cuthbert's Church, in conjunction with the parish council and with help from myself, therefore decided to open a day centre in the church hall. A three-course lunch and afternoon tea were provided at cost price, while we listened to the health problems of those who attended, their mental and social needs. Gradually we were able to build up a team of professionals, often working on a session basis. Like all small voluntary projects, we also had to listen to the needs of staff. This was an essential part of the process if team members were to be freed to listen to the needs of those visiting the centre.

In the early 1990s I was invited by The World Council of Churches (WCC) to be a consultant to their HIV/AIDS unit, to be involved in providing educational material and services for developing countries in the so-called Third World, who were the worst affected by this disease that was fast becoming a pandemic. The aim was to develop an understanding of this growing problem, by offering local, regional and national education via the churches, and by putting on conferences in countries that had neither sufficient educational material nor facilities for the prevention of further infection. Through the auspices of the

WCC we visited the Caribbean, India and Thailand – as well as South Africa, Bishop Desmond Tutu having invited me to arrange a four-day conference for all his clergy in the Cape Town area. We went to Brazil, where we helped set up an HIV/AIDS centre in Recife and held conferences in other major cities. I was invited to Australia to launch the first conference for clergy on HIV/AIDS in Melbourne, and this was followed by similar talks to clergy in Sydney and Newcastle.

In all these places, there was disagreement on the issue of sexual activity outside marriage, while homosexuality was more often than not seen as the greatest sin. The following statement is just an example of the views expressed: 'The Bible clearly states this to be so it deserves God's punishment – they deserve the disease, death and the damnation of hell.' I never allowed myself to become involved in such theological discussions. I would simply state, 'I suspect that one day we shall all know which interpretation of the Bible is correct, compassion or condemnation.' This work involved hearing through listening to people, paying attention to the structures and the communities within which they lived, worked and existed in various states of poverty.

Our listening will differ between persons, as between communities and nations. Whatever the situation, we are all attempting to hear through the depth of our listening, as we take on the challenges of opening our ears so that we may enable the other person to inwardly hear his or her way forward into a life worth living and dying for.

8

The priesthood of all believers

I am a link in a chain, a bond of connection between persons. He has not created me for naught. I shall do good, I shall do his work; I shall be an angel of peace, a preacher of truth in my own place, while not intending it, if I do but keep his commandments and serve Him in my calling.

John Henry Newman

I firmly believe I have been called into the priesthood. I was baptised, confirmed, and finally ordained. On the day of my ordination into the diaconate, Bishop Everard Lunt gave me a signed copy of the New Jerusalem Bible inscribed with the following quote from St Paul, suggested as a guideline to my ministry: 'Keep as your pattern the sound teaching you have heard from me [Paul], in faith and love that are in Christ Jesus. You have been entrusted to look after something precious; guard it with the help of the Holy Spirit who lives in us.' This I have attempted to do, with help from all those who have in one way or another ministered to me. Thankfully only my Creator will be able to assess this ministry, freely offered, thanks be to God.

In my first homily after being priested by Bishop Trevor Huddleston in 1970, I used the following quote from *The Divine Milieu* by Pierre Teilhard de Chardin:

To the full extent of my power, *because I am a priest*, I wish from now on to be the first to become conscious of all that the world loves, pursues and suffers; I want to be the first to seek, to sympathise and to suffer; the first to open myself out and sacrifice myself – to become more widely human and more nobly of the earth than any of the world's events.

Bishop Huddleston reminded me that 'the call to the priesthood is the call "to love one another as I have and *do love you*." ' We do so knowing that we love with the love of God all those who love us, and nurtured by the fact that we are unafraid of loving ourselves, of being open to loving others, embraced as we are by the eternal love of God.

For the priest, God's love is and must be central to his or her whole being, warts and all. God's willing love is the touchstone of one's life and ministry, is its driving force and inspiration through the gift of the Holy Spirit of divine loving.

The Nature of Priesthood

There are many definitions of priesthood; I suspect that every priest will have his or her own definition and experience. For me it is 'being there' with deep concern for all who come into my orbit of concern, with their differing needs. I pray for them and myself from within the stillness of silence embracing me.

Nowhere in the New Testament is the Christian minister referred to as a priest, although the word had entered the Christian vocabulary as a description of ministry by the time of Polycrates of Ephesus in AD 190. Priesthood is rooted in the most ancient religious consciousness of humanity before it became specifically Christian. Within the Anglican ordinal the priest is seen in a threefold way: as watchman, messenger and steward.

I believe being ordained as a deacon and priest initially comes through a personal call, demanding a personal response nurtured by the 'spirit of sacrifice' and the 'essential mark of the inwardness of priesthood'. Ken Leech reminds us that 'priesthood is not a job but an *identity*, a condition, a sacramental state, one cannot shed it or be rid of it, though one may cease to practise certain functions associated with it. *The priest is ordained for ever*' (Leech, *Spirituality and Pastoral Care*, p. 127).

It is crucial that the priest must first of all be humanly human, unafraid to be the truth of herself. We are all called to be open to the mystery of Jesus' life and ministry; to be vulnerably open, in contact, and supportive of all manner of people, with innumerable dimensions of individual and other situations, as was Jesus.

There is no doubt that the very soul of the priest's life is her relationship with God. It is a relationship deep, strong, utterly human and all-embracing of self and others. I believe that the ministry of the minister comprises four basic functions working in conjunction with each other, although one or other of these may be more prominent depending on the person's needs and situation. These four functions, I suggest, are: Prayer – Pastor – Priest – Prophet.

Prayer is a continuing love affair with God, for all God's peoples and the all of creation. Being in the silent depths of listening enables us to hear. I believe it is central to all other aspects of the minister's work of being there for others. True prayer is simply 'being there' and available towards nurturing the various ministries of the minister.

Pastor – to be a pastor is to be involved in the practical aspects of ministry, offering differing services according to the needs of the individual, the group, the parish, the local and wider ministry.

Priest – to be a priest is to carry out the sacramental aspects of ministry in awareness of the fact that priesthood belongs to everyone. The man or woman as priest will be in the sacred work of celebrating and offering the Eucharist (the Mass), being ready to hear confession and offer God's blessing, fully aware of the fact that he or she too falls short of the mark through his or her own imperfections.

Prophet – to be a prophet is to be called to be a listener who hears himself into the very depths of the soul, not only one's own soul but also those of others: the parish, the community, the soul of humanity and, I suggest, the soul of God nurturing the soul of all creation.

Monica Furlong writes as follows about the qualities she looks for in a priest: 'I want them to be people who are secure enough in the value of what they are doing to have time to read, to sit and think, and who can face the emptiness and possible depression which often attacks people when they do not keep the surface of their mind occupied' (quoted in Leech, *Spirituality and Pastoral Care*, p. 130).

Prayer

Prayer in its differing modes is the very soul of the varied ministries of priesthood, all of which are nurtured by prayer, meditation and contemplation within the awesome stillness of silence. Prayer, for Jesus, was the wellspring of his entire ministry and so it must be for all ministers, whatever their label. Prayer is the gateway to a deepening of one's spirituality, the springboard of compassion. Thomas Merton would say that 'contemplative-action' is the bedrock nurturing the ministry that does not know how to reject and is open to all. As Bishop Michael Ramsey reminded ordinands, deacons and priests throughout his ministry, their 'prime work is that of prayer with its own intensity of sorrow and joy'. For me prayer is an ongoing activity. It is, if you like, my soul praying into the soul of God. I see that the great mystery for every person is that we are born into the soul of our lives when we are conceived and as we emerge, not only from the womb of our mother, but also from the womb of God, the eternal Father and Mother of all people.

Prayer can more often than not be offered through the senses of hearing, seeing, touching, smelling and tasting. Our senses are there to enable us to enjoy and to care for ourselves, others and creation in all its awesomeness. Such care is, or can be, a spiritual experience par excellence, delicate and yet so powerful that we are left in the mystery of wonder beyond the non-words of silence. The basic truth about prayer is that none of us can ever move into its mystery without taking others with us. Is this not what we are doing at intercessions, whether in the privacy of our cell, our space within the flat or home, during the Eucharist or at other services? Usually they include the whole community of God's people, of all faiths and of none. Prayer connects – it's as simple as that; it allows us to connect with God's connecting and holding all creation together.

The way of prayer ideally is the way of revolution via revelation. As Henri Nouwen reminds us,

> Is there a third way, a Christian way? It is my growing con-
> viction that in Jesus the mystical and the revolutionary
> ways are not opposites, but two sides of the same human
> mode of experiential transcendence. I am increasingly

convinced that conversion is the individual equivalent of revolution. (Nouwen, *The Wounded Healer*, p. 19)

Whenever I hear or read the word revolution, I want to put alongside it revelation, that arises through the stillness of silence, embraced by hope. For me revolution without revelatory truth can have very negative results. I suggest this is what Nouwen means when he writes,

> Therefore every real revolutionary is challenged to be a mystic at heart, and he [or she] who walks the mystical [i.e. revelatory] way is called to unmask the illusory quality of human society. Mysticism and revolution [tempered by revelation] are two aspects of the same attempt to bring about a radical change. No mystic can prevent him or herself from becoming a social critic, since in self-reflection he [or she] will discover the roots of a sick society, no revolutionary can avoid facing his or her own human condition, since in the midst of their struggle for a new world they will find that they are also fighting their own reactionary fears and false ambitions. (ibid.)

Basic Priesthood

The priest is the person who has become humanly sacramental, having been caught up in the mystery, the offerings of Jesus the Christ and of individual persons unique in their dignity of difference and innerness so often hidden within the various pains and fears of life, within life's ordinariness.

The priest who celebrates the Eucharist is to become a eucharistic person, a walking sacrament of Christ's sacrifice. As in the Eucharist there is both awe and intimacy, so in priestly life there is both an exalted dignity and a common humanity. Yet the priest is also a vulnerably broken human being; it is this vulnerability that 'lies at the heart of effective priesthood' (Leech, *Spirituality and Pastoral Care*, p. 135).

William Countryman writes – and I agree with him – that it is crucial for us to recognise and accept the very real fact that 'there are two, distinct but related priesthoods that co-exist in the life of the Church – the fundamental human priesthood and the sacramental counterpart, the priesthood of religion' (Country-man, *Living on the Border of the Holy*, p. xi). I prefer the term 'basic priesthood', as the word 'fundamental' is so closely related to the fundamentalism that is threatening to split the Church. In quoting the author I will use his word – although mentally replacing it with 'basic priesthood':

> The fundamental priesthood belongs to all of us by virtue of our humanity. The only preparations or authorisation for it is what comes from living our common human life honestly and attentively in the presence of the Holy. ... We need to remember Jesus' priesthood belonged to the fundamental priesthood of all humanity, not to the sacramental priest-hood of ancient Israel or to the later church. He did not found or belong to any priesthood of religion except in the iconic sense that he was a maverick rabbi. (ibid., pp. 33, 61)

I have an inner sense that the fundamental (basic) priesthood of all believers is nurtured by love's compassion and vision. And it may, with the courage of faith, be prepared to evolve in so doing and become the true pioneer of change towards initiating the priesthood of *all humanity*. This appears to me to be the natural way forward: that in time the priesthood of all believers will become the priesthood of all humanity, nurtured by the spirituality and the innate priesthood of compassion, linked as they are to the eternal spirituality of God's unending love for all humanity and indeed all creation.

It saddens me that women *still* do not have complete access to the sacramental priesthood. This is also true of gay men, unless they live celibate or chaste lives. Those who are unable to live such lives, but who rather strive to live with the integrity of their committed relationship, physically, mentally, socially and spiritually, as baptised members within the priesthood of all believers, risk being rejected. To be unable to live this truth is to diminish their co-creative potential. It is also to devalue one of the greatest of gifts from our Creator, offered to all whatever their gender or sexual orientation. The Church's teaching denies its claim to be 'inclusive'. It has forgotten that Jesus was not a fundamentalist but was utterly inclusive. Jesus was an outsider who suffered abuse and mortal wounding. His suffering became the soul and inspiration for his followers, that they might continue his ministry to 'in-gather' all through uninhibited acceptance rather than rejection. We need to accept the fact that we are all imperfect; this is equally so for the Church – that is, the Christian Movement, symbolic of the body and love of Jesus who is now the Christ for all – whose co-creative potential hangs in the balance between rejection and acceptance. The question is, what would the Church have accomplished without the millions of men and women whose strength has been nurtured through their vulnerability? Those women and men have been and still are the backbone, at the very edge and yet at the very heart of the Christian Movement that is the Church, symbolic of the ministry and the compassionate love of Jesus throughout the centuries.

Thornton Wilder has said: 'without your wounds where would your power be? ... The very angels themselves cannot persuade the wretched and blundering children of the earth as can one human being broken on the wheels of living. In Love's service, only the wounded soldiers can serve' (Wilder, *The Angel that Troubled the Waters*, 1928). The following words by William Countryman will surprise many, and yet there is a great truth within them:

> The priesthood of humanity requires no ordination. This priesthood is the priesthood of Christian laity – not in the sense of belonging exclusively to nonclerics, but in the sense of being the priesthood of the *laos*, that is, the whole people of God. Ordination does not and cannot add anything to it, for it is the priesthood of Christ himself. It is our fundamental priesthood lived out on the common human borders of the TRANSCENDENT. It is the priesthood after the order of Melchizedek. It is not preparatory to some other, higher priesthood. It does not step back for some 'better' priesthood to arrive on the scene. *There is no better priesthood.* As I have already said, ordination simply creates a sacramental model, a religious icon that reminds us who we are and points us towards the living out of our priesthood.
>
> (Countryman, *Living on the Border of the Holy*, pp. 86–7)

The author demonstrates to me the very simple fact that Jesus – the Jewish non-priest – is the source of both the fundamental (basic) priesthood and the sacramental priesthood that excludes no one. It calls upon all of us to live more fully as persons with a deepening spirituality, with a sense of compassion linked to an awesome wonder and appreciation of every person's unique dignity. Whether Christian or not, we are all the sons and daughters of God; equally we are sisters and brothers within the rainbow community of all God's people and the all of creation in its smallness and its largeness. We are each one of us a mystery within the greater mystery of all creation and the ultimate mystery of God.

I firmly believe in the realistic concept of 'The priesthood of all believers'; all those baptised, preferably as adults, are essential for becoming members of this basic priesthood. Having been baptised myself as an adult, with some awareness of the rites and their inner meanings, I believe it is this basic rite that nurtures all other Christian rites. When I was a novice I remember being at the final profession and the first profession of two Franciscan Brothers. Sitting next to me was a perpetual postulant, a former bishop, who refused to be professed. He said to me at the time, 'I don't know why all the fuss, the Christian rite of baptism was initiated by Jesus, and all other rites flowed from this. The Reformation made quite clear that the baptised person was initiated into "the priesthood of all believers", one that was different and more inclusive than the Temple priesthood of the Jewish people.'

Throughout my life, in particular when I was a nurse prior to being ordained, I have attempted to offer the fourfold actions within the priesthood of prayer, pastor, priest and prophet. This ministry has been nurtured by innumerable people who have allowed me to share in their differing joy and pain, their hopes and sadness and their search for a way to realise their potential. It is my acceptance of their uniqueness and dignity, their concern and their hope for a life worth living that affirms for me that all persons baptised – in the name of the Father–Mother, the Son of service, and the Holy Spirit of divine loving – together live, move and have their being within the priesthood of all believers. This fundamental (basic) priesthood of all believers is linked into the ongoing, evolving and compassionate ministry of Jesus the Christ. Thanks be to God for this evolving ministry and the enriching of my life. Amen.

9

Spirituality

> *Spirituality is the very breath of the inner life. It is an essential resource in the transformation of consciousness on our planet, and it will be enormously beneficial in our attempts to build a new universal society. Spirituality, intermysticism and interspirituality can clear a path for a return of the sacred in a wider culture.*
>
> Wayne Teasdale, *The Mystic Heart*, p. 249

Spirituality is a difficult word to define. What do we mean by it? There are probably as many different interpretations of the word and its meaning as there are people discussing it, writing books about it, giving conferences and retreats on it. I like to think that spirituality is a way of life, and that how we make this life is what spirituality is all about. We continue this journey in the awareness that no one way or manual will provide the definitive guide for evolving into inner life. We have all been created for our own uniquely personal journey and we are willing to take full responsibility for doing so. We are unafraid of using the differing resources available to us from other faith traditions, in the awareness that we are part of a common heritage. Our journey is our own, not one copied from another person's journey. We are delighted that there are no two persons, no two souls alike.

I, along with millions of others, sense that we are all spiritual. We may not be aware of it, we may not even like the idea of it. I believe, however, that spiritual potential is seeded within all people. To be caught up in the spirituality of life is to be caught up in a practical, mystical and universal understanding of spirituality. Evelyn Underhill defines spirituality in its purest form as 'the science of ultimates, the science of union with the Absolute, and nothing else ... the mystic is the person who attains to this union, not the person who talks about it. Not to know about, but to Be is the mark of the real initiate' (Underhill, *Mysticism*, p. 72).

I have a deep sense that mysticism is the womb of both religion and spirituality. They are the means by which we may directly experience the Holy. For Christians, the Holy is union and communion with God, the ultimate creator and lover of all creations creating.

Mysticism has the ability to inform us that we are all individual members of the community of all God's peoples. There is a growing awareness within many people that a new interspiritual and intermystical age is being birthed within the pain and chaos of today's world, echoing in a way Julian of Norwich's great statement that 'all shall be well, all manner of things shall be well'.

The interspiritual and intermystical age

Wayne Teasdale, author of *The Mystic Heart*, writing on what he calls 'The Interspiritual Age', reminds us that we are at the dawn of a new consciousness, 'a radically fresh approach to our life as the human family in a fragile world'. He sees this birth into a new awareness in a number of shifts in our understanding, which he details as follows:

- The emergence of ecological awareness and sensitivity to the natural, organic world, with an acknowledgement of the basic fragility of the earth
- A growing sense of the rights of other species
- A recognition of the interdependence of all domains of life and reality
- The ideal of abandoning a militant nationalism as a result of this tangible sense of our interdependence
- A deep, evolving experience of community between and among the religions through their individual members
- A growing receptivity to the inner treasures of the world's religions
- An openness to the cosmos with the realisation that the relationship between humans and the earth is part of the larger community of the universe.

These combine towards a growing awareness that:

> Each one of these shifts represents dramatic change; taken together, they will define the thought and culture of the third millennium. Fewer and fewer people are questioning the vital importance of environmental issues. Their significance is so great that Thomas Berry – who refers to himself as a *geo-logian*, or a theologian for the earth – believes in naming this new period in history the *Ecological or Ecozoic Age*. We could really name the age after any of these shifts in understanding. To encompass them all, however, perhaps the best name for this new segment of historical experience is the *Interspiritual Age*. (Teasdale, *The Mystic Heart*, pp. 4–5)

I believe that today we are being caught up in a battle of attitudes, the negative and the positive, and at times it certainly appears as though the latter are losing. Yet today there are positive ways to more co-creative sharing and understanding, with acceptance of the revelation of an emerging 'Consciousness Revolution'. Today there is a deep and growing individual and collective questioning of what life is all about. Who are we? Why are we here? What is our real purpose and what is it we want? The same questioners are looking beyond materialistic and consumerist cultures for a deeper sense of meaning and purpose. They are searching for an inner peace and a way to nurture their spiritual hunger. If we are to assist in the healing of the planet, this will occur only with a change of consciousness, through having freed ourselves from our egocentricity, from our attachments to things, self-centredness, and through having become more caring, compassionate and loving towards ourself and others. Clearly these transformations call for an inner self-awakening, through a rising of consciousness within ourselves and others.

The development of this new interspiritual and intermystical age will depend upon our willingness to meet the needs of the necessary shifts for nurturing the consciousness revolution that is emerging in today's world. This will require new approaches to a spirituality that will transcend a religious culture of fragmentation and isolationism. There are many echoes in the world that the direct experience of interspirituality and the intermystical will pave the way for a new universal view of mysticism, which is the common heart-soul of humanity. From a Christian point of view I have always felt that the growth, the renewal of spirituality will come about through small cells of Christians sharing their insights with those of other faiths, thereby empowering each of us towards a fuller understanding and growth within our particular faith journey. Ideally these interfaith cells or groups would also welcome others of no faith, whose questioning would sharpen for us a deeper awareness of the meaning of our differing faith journeys.

This movement would evolve through an ongoing dialogue and communion with everything of value in our different religious and mystical traditions, promoting the dignity and integrity of all persons through our differing spiritualities.

> *How* we make this journey is what spirituality is really about. No manual for the inner life fits the need of all people. Finding our own path is part of what it means to have a *measure* of independence and *inner* directedness. In the English mystical tradition, there is a wonderful saying, "Pray as you can, not as you can't". This means finding the right way for you to relate to the divine, this is what prayer helps us to do. (Teasdale, *The Mystic Heart*, p. 18)

The emergence of communities between and among differing faith religions and various native cultures around the planet, their growing discovery of one another, is a crucial and vital component of interspirituality. Our active commitment to this larger community is itself a new type of spirituality. All those who are committed and working in this evolving interspiritual community are actually – whether we are aware of it or not – engaged in developing a new form of spiritual life that embraces the oneness and the innerness of life for all. Andrew Harvey, in his book *The Essential Mystics*, outlines for us the commonality within the differing faiths in a helpful way:

1. Taoism: The Way of Tao – Way of Final Reality, of the Universe and of Authentic Human Life. (p. 17)
2. Hinduism: The Way of Presence – Presence of Pure Being, Pure Consciousness and Pure Bliss (p. 35)

3. Buddhism: The Way of Charity – of Analysis to help human beings attain their final freedom to live in the light of Compassion (p. 67)

4. Judaism: The Way of Holiness – offering affirmative vision of the Divine, of human glory and glory of all creation. (p. 87)

5. Ancient Greece: The Way of Beauty – Genius for scientific skepticism, rational inquiry and philosophical humanism. (p. 111)

6. Islam: The Way of Passion – that peace comes when one' s entire being and life are surrendered to God. (p. 137)

7. Christianity: The Way of Love-in-Action – embodying the truth of the other mystical traditions reflected in the depth of the Christian message. (p. 169)

(Taken from Harvey, *The Essential Mystics*)

Wayne Teasdale maintains, and I believe he is right in saying so, that:

> Third Millennial spirituality will also be interspirituality and intermystical. It will be an enhanced understanding of the inner life through assimilating the psychological, moral, aesthetic, spiritual, and literary treasures of the world's religions. Each tradition will define itself in relation to every other viable tradition of the inner life; each will take into account the totality of the spiritual journey – all the forms it assumes in human experience.
>
> (Teasdale, *The Mystic Heart*, p. 238)

This means there will be no proselytising and each member will mirror her specific faith in nurturing and enriching her own life. It will release an awareness of the uniqueness of each person's faith journey, to be respected as we journey together towards the holy centre that embraces all God's people of every faith and of none. The process will be encouraged through our recognition and acceptance that:

> Interspirituality is a commitment to this enhanced vision. It is no longer content to embrace one tradition alone, no matter how admirable. Interspirituality, as intermysticism,

seeks the larger understanding of spirituality itself and will not settle for anything less. Intermysticism is the realisation that there is one universal tradition of the mystical life with many branches. All of them are relevant and have a perennial value. If we are truly *intermystics*, we are open to wisdom wherever we find it. (ibid.)

I believe Christians and others would accept the fact that spirituality is the very breath of the inner life, nurturing and responding to everyday events in our outer lives. If we are to be involved in transforming consciousness in our lives, the planet and the cosmos, we may only attempt to do so knowing we are all linked into the awesome majesty of God's creation. We are also linked in differing ways as we work towards the up-building of a new universal society. Through the combined energies of spirituality, intermysticism and interspirituality, this work will have a good chance of succeeding. Together these energies will help us to clear a pathway of information, directing us all, of whatever culture, towards a greater awareness of the sacred mystery.

The spirituality of sexuality

I believe that anyone involved in the sacred ministry of listening must be totally aware of their sexuality as well as their spirituality, recognising both as being essential for a fully lived life nurtured by the goodness of self-love. The fullness of one without the other may very well lead to an unfulfilled life.

Christianity owes its origin to the Word that 'was made flesh and dwelt among us' (John 1:14). Here love is humanised through being fleshed out in our lives. This love is to be experienced and lived through the gifts of sex: our sexual orientation, our eroticism, and our spirituality. There is no doubt that sexual health and spiritual health are linked; both sexual integrity and spiritual wholeness are required if committed relationships are to be both nurturing and co-creative of each other.

Spirituality is a capacity rather than an actuality. We are first and foremost a spiritual species, due to the fact that the physical world to which we belong is embodied in the spiritual world of creation. Spirituality is the attempt to live our lives to the full, in such a way that they will encourage others to realise that to be spiritual is to be fully alive to life and our differing co-creative potential.

The spiritual life involves our exploration of life in all its fullness, including the 'spirituality of our imperfections' that in some mysterious way nurtures our journey into the mystery of death and of life. This insight allows us to acknowledge the fact that our spiritualities enable transformational changes. It is through the acceptance of the gifts of our differing spiritualities and spiritual orientations that we are enabled to accept our becoming who we are in truth.

'Sex' itself is biologically based. It involves all the wondrous biological and genital characteristics of the human body and is orientated towards both procreation and co-creation, for pleasure, for the release of tension and loneliness. We might describe it as the body's gift of sacred pleasure. Basically it is the inner drive, driven by a longing for connection, for affirmation of one's self, of others and of creation. It can also, however, be perceived negatively and this in turn can lead to fear and a denial of one's sexuality.

The word 'erotic' comes from the Greek *eros* (desire). Like most words that refer to sexual realities, eros has been understood in different ways throughout history. The tension between eros as a physical drive and as a spiritual energy is as old as human memory. But for now, we will use the term 'erotic' to mean the sacred attraction to beauty and deep desire for fulfilment in all aspects of life. Rollo May describes eros as 'the drive towards union with what we belong to' (quoted in Sheldrake, *Befriending our Desires*, p. 58). William McNamara, the hermit monk, in describing what he means by the word erotic, speaks of its radical sense as 'a reaching and stretching with every fibre of one's body-person for the fullness of life' (McNamara, *Mystical Passion*, p. 8). It is that energy that sends one towards the other, while at the same time sending oneself into the mystery that is beyond everything. If you like, it is the peak of a spiritual experience, if we see it as that energy that lifts us out of our self within the presence of another who is also being sent into the mystery of love.

Sensuality, the companion of sexuality, is related to the notion of 'sense' and sense experience. If it is left at that, and if sexuality is used merely in a physical way, then we are no more than physical beings. But our sensuality can also be a bridge between our sexual and spiritual selves. We need to be brought together in some form of harmony, otherwise we fail to develop the fullness of our potential. Sensuality is about being open to experiencing fully our senses of hearing, touching, seeing, smelling and tasting in our loving of each other. The more we are alive to ourselves, to others and creation, the more we are open to spirituality, and the more we shall be open to the gifts of our sexuality and orientation.

Our sexual orientations are not of our choosing. They are gifts from our creator, to be fully integrated into our lives. Most of us have never chosen our gender, our sexuality, be we hetero-sexual, non-heterosexual, bisexual, transvestite or transsexual. The percentage who do so is, I believe, very small. But we do remember when we discovered the truth of our sexual orienta-tion, to be honoured as a vital aspect of our lives. Sexuality is love energy. It refers to the spiritual, emotional, physical, psychological, social and cultural aspects of relating to one another as embodied male and female persons, created in the image of God. It has more to do with being co-creative than pro-creative. It has to do with total offering and receiving. Our differing sexualities and orientations are for the uniting of body, mind, and soul.

We should never be afraid of our sexualities or orientations. They are the raw material for nurturing our wholeness potential.

> The fact of our sexualities is that whatever they are, what-ever their style, whatever the source or cause of our turn-ons, it isn't our fault. Our sexualities are, for the most part, fully developed by the time we emerge from puberty and there wasn't a lot we could have done about them along the way. We are not responsible for the bodies with which we are born, for the way in which our libidos separated, from our childhood, or that society that shaped and formed us. There is no point in beating ourselves up about our sexualities, however unusual or antisocial. We had not the capacity to control the process through which they came.
>
> (Ind, *Memories of Bliss*, p. 97)

There is no doubt that for some time to come there will be sexual dilemmas for individuals, for those whose role is to listen, for community and the churches. Whatever the dilemmas, the various issues regarding our sexualities demand the courage of truth and justice in both individual and corporate responses. The Christian man or woman might well come to his or her personal truth by asking the following questions: What does it mean to be loving of self? What does it mean to be loving of my partner, family members, and friends? What does it mean to be loving of the person I do not get on with, the person I fear? What does it mean to be loving of Jesus, the Christ? What does it mean to be loving of God, my Creator, whatever my gender or sexual orientation?

What is sexuality?

> Something which existed from the beginning,
> That we have heard
> And have seen with our own eyes;
> That we have watched
> And touched with our hands ... (1 John 1:1, NIV)

Although the various definitions of spirituality within the literature are diverse and varied, there is one common theme that runs through most attempts to tie it down: the significance of human relationships, love and commitment, as gateways to spiritual fulfilment. Relationships with a higher power or with other human beings form the intractable core of human spirituality. Although spirituality can find expression in the experience of beauty, and of art and music, it is primarily through our relationships with one another and, for some people, with God, that we are able to grasp and experience a sense of love, hope, meaning, value, purpose, and connectedness. It is only as we enter into meaningful relationships with others and find ourselves loved and affirmed, that we can begin to understand what it means to care and accept that we are worthy of being loved and cared for.

The Spirituality of Friendship

The Gospel proclaims, 'God is love'. We might just as easily say, 'God is friendship'. Jesus clearly emphasised friendship with his disciples: 'I shall no longer call you servants ... I call you friends.' The prime source of celebration in life for me is that of friendship. This is the most human and sacred relationship. Friendship never just happens. The seedling of friendship must be given space and time to mature. It begins with recognition of a shared stillness within. It appears as if from nowhere and yet there is a recognition of a hidden past being awakened to new life. It is as though two souls recognise each other at an unexpected meeting of a kind that will open the way towards the renewal of friendship. It is as though the exile of loneliness is over in the awareness that there is more than just a mutual presence of one to the other.

In the Celtic tradition there is a beautiful understanding of love and friendship. One of the fascinating ideas is that of 'soul love'. In this book I have already several times used the term 'soul friend'. The old Gaelic term for this is *anam cara* – *anam* is the Gaelic word for soul and *cara* is the word for friend. With our Anam Cara, our soul friend, we share our innermost heart and mind. This friendship was an act of recognition and belonging. Your friendship cuts across all convention, morality and category. It implies that, through a true friendship, we are linked to an ancient and eternal way with the friend of our soul; drawn together by the divine energy that flows between two friends from a source beyond their comprehension.

When old friends meet again there is a touch of expectancy as soul meets with soul, with all they are for each other. These are friendships of love, which enable one human presence to meet co-creatively with another at the threshold where divine and human presence ebb and flow into each other. A friendship of love is ready to reach out towards others and draw them in. Such a friendship is nurtured by the fact that its subjects matter to each other and to any other person who comes into its enlarging circle. The greatest gift we may offer to another is the first of ourselves, with no strings attached. We do so in the awareness that friendship is about 'bonding' rather than 'binding'. Its main gift is nurtured by the spiritualities of friendship. It is very affirming and reminds us of how we relate to our perception of truth and goodness as friends one to another. In this way we enable each other to celebrate lives worth living and dying for.

John O'Donohue, in his book *Anam Cara*, reminds us, 'you can never love another person unless you are equally involved in the beautiful, but difficult, spiritual work of learning to love yourself. There is within each of us at the soul level an enriching fountain of love. In other words, you do not have to go outside yourself to know what love is' (O'Donohue, *Anam Cara*, p. 50).

God is friendship – we are born and nurtured into that friendship through each other.

10
Solitude and silence

There is nothing in this world that proclaims the grandeur and beauty of life on earth more eloquently than silence.

Roger Housden

The cave of the heart is solitude. We are drawn towards this solitude for a variety of reasons: to escape the excessive noise of modern society, its stresses and pain, perhaps even to escape ourselves. Gradually we become aware of the benefit of finding time for ourselves as persons, a time of quiet solitude for body, mind and soul within the healing space of silence.

> Solitude is a door. When you open the door to solitude, you may find another door behind it. That is the door of silence. Silence, too, is an environment for prayer. In silence we put ourselves in touch with God and also our deeper selves. Thoughts long buried come to the surface and long repressed feelings bubble up. Silence exposes certain issues within our lives and almost without effort. What is important comes to the forefront. Now we can place the 'most important issue' before God as we pray.
>
> (Griffin, *Doors into Prayer*, p. 35)

Henri Nouwen in his book *The Way of the Heart* writes about how necessary solitude is for our inner growth. But equally he points out how solitude is misunderstood in today's society:

> We say to each other that we crave solitude in our lives. What we really are thinking of however is a time and a place for ourselves in which we are not bothered by other people, can think our own thoughts, express our own complaints, and do our own thing, whatever it may be. For us,

solitude most often means privacy. ... But that is not the solitude of St John The Baptist, of St Anthony or St Benedict, Charles de Foucauld or the Brothers of Taizé. For them solitude is not a private therapeutic place. Rather, it is a place of conversion, the place where the old self dies and a new self is born, the place where the emergence of the new man and the new woman occurs.

(Nouwen, *The Way of the Heart*, p. 18)

The way that solitude might lead us into the holy sanctum is through acceptance and commitment to the workings of silence by simply being in that space, taking quality time 'to be' in the silence that beckons us. We can ask ourselves, what is the difference between silence and solitude?

Silence is sometimes defined as 'the condition of no sound'. Solitude, on the other hand, is a deeper, richer experience. ... I can have silence without solitude, but I cannot have solitude without being silent on some level. It is a necessary prerequisite. Most people are uncomfortable with silence, and subconsciously avoid it. But those who long for a state of solitude when they pray must first become accustomed to silence. (Thibodeaux, *Armchair Mystic*, p. 41)

Howard Cooper reminds us that 'silence is frightening. It throws us back on ourselves. It presents us with our solitariness, our aloneness. We fear that aloneness, confusing it with loneliness' (Cooper, *The Alphabet of Paradise*, p. 131). The unsettling question – 'Why are you here? What are you doing here?' – is one any of us might have to face were we to allow silence into our lives, and allow the silence to speak. But this enquiry is what we fear' (ibid., p. 134). I suggest that to fear silence is to fear life. I wonder how many of us have taken the time to ask ourselves, where do all the outer sounds come from? I suggest they come from the cave of silence, if you like from the heart of silence. Eckhart Tolle asks us, 'Do you hear the dog barking in the distance? Listen carefully. Can you feel the presence of the Unmanifested in that? You can't. Look for it in the silence out of which sounds come and into which they return. Paying attention to outer silence creates inner silence: The mind becomes still. A portal is opening' (Tolle, *The Power of Now*, p. 112).

I am fully aware that my spiritual growth is daily nurtured through my time of being in the silence, in the solitude of just 'being there' in the presence of God, the wonder that permeates my life and ministry. When I read the following words by Howard Cooper, I felt they should be in this book – they are so real, so meaningful, so true to my own experiences of being in the silences of life.

> There are few axioms ... in regard to spiritual practice. But here I want to risk one. *There can be no spiritual growth without silence.* Although we have come to depend on external stimulation to keep us going, our souls need respite from the ceaseless clamour of the world. Absence of silence stifles our spiritual growth: without the space to be quietly attentive to what is going on inside us, our capacity for reflective spiritual being is stunted. The rush of life drowns out the still small voice within.
>
> (Cooper, *The Alphabet of Paradise*, p. 133)

Thanks for taking that risk.

The nothingness of silence contains the mystery of words – enriched through emerging from within the womb of silence. Throughout the centuries the spiritual and ascetic traditions and the various faith communities have recognised the fact that silence is crucial to an authentic spiritual and prayer life:

> In order to listen we need silence; we also need interior silence, nurturing each other. 'Interior silence' has a long spiritual history. It is the silence practised by hesychasts in their search for unification of the heart; it is the silence of the monastic tradition, it is the silence of the prayer of adoration of God's presence; it is the silence treasured by mystics of every religious tradition; it is the silence that saturates poetic language, the silence that is the substance of music, the silence that is essential to hearing. When inhibited by silence the body becomes a revelation of the person. ... Who is the crucified Christ if not the icon of silence, the silence of God himself – the silence of the moment of the cross is able

to express the inexpressible; the image of the invisible God found in a man nailed to the cross. The silence of the cross is the authoritative source from which every theological word should be drawn.

(Enzio Bianchi, *Words of Spirituality*, p. 74)

Thoughts on spiritual reading

I suggest that spiritual reading is reading in depth. It is listening with the inner ear through the many layers of meaning. Slow meditative reading, both of the Bible and other faith scriptures, is a reminder to me of the fact that there is ultimately one inspirer of the differing faith scriptures, that they all point to God our ultimate creator. I sense that through these scriptures God is offering differing insights and pathways for spiritual growth. I believe that the growing interfaith movement is demonstrating an acknowledgement that each of these insights enriches the specific pathways its members take. I am, or at least I endeavour to be, a Christian strong enough in the faith to be able to listen and take notice of other faiths and in so doing to have my Christian faith enriched.

I have a flexible plan of reading. For me the ideal starting place is a simple prayer: 'May I be ready for the mystery hidden in the words, as I read with an open heart, and a silence that impregnates my soul and my covenant of service.' It is through reading and meditating on 'the word' that I meet the essence of the people in the Bible and their experiences of life; their soul's anguish and confusion; the wonder of creation and the celebration of their differing cultures; their wars and their famines; their life and the stories of their differing communities and spiritualities.

For me the Bible comes alive when I read it slowly and with a sense of mystery, as well as an awareness of the fact that no one individual or school of thought has the edge on meaning, on interpretation; and the spiritual, social cultures of the day at best are insights as to how we might learn from their wisdom.

The question today is, 'How do I, and others, hear the voice of God through reading the Word of God?' It is important, indeed it helps me, to recognise that most people in the Bible, in 'falling short of the mark', have been subject to weaknesses similar to those which we ourselves are all too prone to, living as we do with the spirituality of our various imperfections. The Bible is a book of personal and corporate stories, of parables as guidelines for growth. It is through the attentiveness of our listening, I believe, that we hear three stories: 'in their story is hidden my story'; 'in my story is hidden their story'; and 'our stories are part of the hidden story of all humanity'.

Timothy Owings speaks of the four traps of prayer into which Bible readers fall. The first is the trap of isolation, 'where an isolated verse is taken here and a verse there, throw them together, and come up with "the way". Taken to its extreme, this is the interpretive method of sectarian religion, cults and religious fanaticism.'

The second trap is the trap of truth finding: 'One approaches the Bible as a treasure chest of "truths" discovered by the faithful. There is no doubt that the Bible is filled with countless truths that confront the reader. The problem lies in the area of method. It is possible to spend a lifetime mining the truths from the Bible and never encounter the reality of God who is the truth of all reality, as revealed in the person of Jesus the Christ who said "I am the Way, the Truth and the Life." '

The third hazard he draws to our attention is the question and answer trap: 'Simply stated, the Bible is God's "answer book" to my questions and problems. While there is a kernel of truth in this, clearly the Bible is not a divine answer book. Yet it does reveal many answers to life's questions. As we read the Bible meditatively and situationally, we discover for ourselves through Bible parables and stories, the poetry and music of the psalms, the hymnbook of the Bible and its teachings, the reality of God who speaks and asks us not a few questions.'

The final snare is the learning-knowledge trap: 'Knowing the facts about the Bible, considering the history of the Bible, even learning well the subject matter within the Bible is not the same as listening to God in the Bible' (Owings, *Hearing God in a Noisy World*, pp. 36–8).

Owings makes very clear the nature of these four traps: isolationism, truth finding, seeking answers to specific questions, and learning-knowledge of the Bible. I must say that at varying times throughout the years I have fallen foul of all four snares, usually when I have not given myself enough time and space to meditate at the depth I should, for various reasons – some genuine and some, I fear, the result of laziness. Still, I have learned through in-depth listening that we have all been gifted to hear and respond to the voice of God, with the hope that it is God we hear and not ourselves projected as God's word.

As a pastoral listener, I am very aware of having evolved into the work of listening to God through simply being in the stillness of no words, in the silence of an embracing presence. In simply 'being there' in this awesome mystery, I sense the wonder of goodness, the hope of love, the truth of justice and the peace of contentment. At other times there is a sense of unease, of indecision, of being in the 'cloud of unknowing', when I am unsure of what is going on with my inner self. During such times, I ask myself, 'Am I looking for answers in the wrong places and am I ready for the reply to my searching?' Or it may be that I say to myself, 'Relax, Bill, be with your inner and outer selves, they are linked. Let go to the "now" moment, let God in, who in fact is already in. Acknowledge it and *let go – let God.'*

The pain of fatigue
Some years ago, while I was working with chemical abusers, a woman called Joan came fairly regularly to see me. Her family history helped me to understand some of the reasons for her drug problems. Her parental history had been identified as being very dysfunctional; her marriage complicated this for her in that her husband, Paul, also came from a difficult family. Both of them had been in various types of therapy since childhood.

One day Joan asked me to become her 'special' friend. I simply asked her 'Why?' Her reply was, 'Because you are a priest.' I discussed this with my supervisor and the psychiatrist attached to the unit; they both felt it might help her, and would enable me to meet her husband. We mutually agreed to meet, initially bi-weekly, for about six months. It was felt that if Joan also wished to write me between visits she could send her letters to me via the unit.

For about six months, it seemed to me that all Joan was doing at each visit was turning on her own inner recording, which kept repeating her early family history. I longed for her to change the inner tape. At times I found myself unable to stay with her, becoming fatigued as I was with the unchanging content of her story. My mind

would wander and I would ask myself how much longer I had to concentrate so attentively on her, her differing movements, her facial
expressions, her tone of voice, the meaning of her silences – though
there were not many – and her story, although I had heard it many
times. I attempted to listen to the differing ways in which it was being
shared and spoken, listening for varying words, anything that might
suggest she was breaking out of her inner prison.

I asked myself, might this be because Joan was awakening in me my
own inner wounds? I further asked myself, 'Why do I feel helpless?'
Could it be due to the fact that she was projecting on to me her own
sense of powerlessness, which prevented her from unlocking the
door of her inner mental prison with her inner key? Maybe Joan had
an inner knowledge, linked to fear, that she would not be able to
cope. Yet, as she was leaving, she would always turn to me and say,
'It's getting easier all the time.' Because I lived in the same area I
often saw her walking down the street, coming towards me on her
way shopping. She would smile and pass on. In those fleeting
moments I saw that her stature was becoming taller and this helped
me to hear her in a completely different way. I sensed she would
eventually be able to unlock her inner prison.

A year later I left the service. I like to think that Joan may have
found a greater sense of love for herself and her family. I also like to
think that she found a greater freedom to accept that, despite what
could not be changed in the circumstances of her traumatic early life
and some of the consequences since, it would be possible to move
on towards realising her fullest potential.

A healthy, realistic and responsible understanding of compassion reminds me, in Henri Nouwen's words, that 'No human
being can understand fully, no human being can give uncondi-
tional love, no human being can offer constant affection, no
human being can enter into the core being and heal our deepest
brokenness. When we forget this and expect more than they can
give we become quickly disillusioned' (Nouwen, *Clowning in
Rome*, p. 41).

11
The listening heart

Our God is a listening God
who hears the cry of the poor,
who bends down and comes to our aid.

Our God calls on each of us to become
a listening heart, attentive to one another
with something of God's own listening heart ...

Donal Harrington

One of the most important words in the spiritual tradition is *ausculta*, which is interpreted as 'listen'. It is the very first word of the Rule of St Benedict. The Benedictine tradition grows out of whole-bodied hearing through listening. The Bible calls responsible listening the first act of obedience to 'the living word of God', and that means far more than merely being nurtured by God's word as food and drink. Through the spiritual discipline of listening, we hear the echoing of God's word in every person, every creature, every movement and stillness that carries the whispers of God towards all he created and knows to be good. Through the gospel we are instructed by listening, feeling the actions of Jesus. This is why it is important that we take time to listen deep within ourselves. It has been said that wisdom consists of hearing the commandments of God, living and being them in the ways of Jesus.

The practice of listening for God within the all of life is based on the perspective of St John's Gospel, and is to be found in various mystical traditions of the Church. The strength of the 'John tradition' is that it produces a spirituality that sees God in all life, and regards all things and all peoples as being inter-related. John's way makes room for an open and therefore an ecumenical – and, I dare to suggest, interfaith – encounter with the 'light of life' wherever it is to be found. In contrast, the strength of the 'Peter tradition' is that it has four walls, as it were; walls that enshrine the light of the truth within the Church, its traditions and sacraments. It is a rock, a place of security and shelter, especially in the midst of stormy change. It allows us, even in our times of great change, of personal confusion, to turn with the faith of hope to the familiar house of prayer and comfort where for centuries successive generations have found truth and guidance.

John and Peter heard the voice of truth through listening in differing ways, and this is why it is important to bring together their differing perspectives and draw on complementary gospel traditions. We need to be reminded that the real cathedral of God is the all of creation. If the churches were to teach this more clearly we might then rediscover the heartbeat of God within every person.

The Bible as a whole offers many clear statements on listening: The Father, Son and Holy Spirit (and I hope the Mother of God) are constantly listening to each other. God listens to the world (Ps. 10:17) and tells the world to listen to his Son (Matt. 17:50). Jesus' mission is that of obedient listening to God's people – to their words and perhaps more importantly into the very depths of their being (John 1:25; Luke 7:39–40). Again we are asked to consider ourselves (Rom. 12:31) by listening to our hearts (Ps. 4:4) and by examining our ways of being (Lam. 3:40). As listeners who hear, we are to be quick to listen to others (Jas. 1:19). We are called to hear through attentive listening, individually and collectively, to the many voices of and in the world. Above all, we are to listen and hear the voice of God, who longs to share himself and his creative ways with us.

Jesus is the prototype of one who listens and hears in depth, thereby enabling him to offer the same quality of listening to others. Christians have a clear mandate for listening and hearing; it is a major theme throughout the Old and New Testaments, and also in the spiritual writings of the desert mothers and fathers, along with the mystics.

Luke's parable of the sower clearly demonstrates the differing levels of listening available to us all if 'we have the ears to listen.' We all have the ears to listen; the question is, do we hear?

Listening to others must begin with listening to ourselves, so that we may learn how to listen to all creatures, creation, and to God, the Father and Mother of all our co-creative endeavours. The Psalmist wrote: 'When you are on your beds, search out your hearts and be silent' (Ps. 4:4). St Paul wrote, 'Think of yourself with sober judgement' (Rom. 12:3). Again, St Paul asks all of us to 'Let God transform you inwardly by a complete change of your mind' (Rom. 12:2).

There is a deep tradition typical of many of the psalms, as our singing voices join in the chorus of the universe, of giving praises to God. This is clearly demonstrated in the last *five* psalms (Pss. 146–150). Some have found it helpful to move into the psalms while listening to the sea, so that their voices might join 'the voices of the waves' and their praises, the praises of 'the ceaseless sea'; others to sing in the night, giving thanks to the stars as the lights of creation.

Throughout the Old Testament, God frequently asks his people to listen to him: 'Listen, Israel: Yahweh your God is the one Yahweh. You shall love Yahweh your God with all your heart, with all your soul, with all your strength' (Deut. 6:4). 'Listen to my voice. Then I shall be your God and you will be my people ' (Jer. 7:23). Samuel acknowledges that he is truly in tune with God: 'Speak, your servant is listening' (1 Sam. 3:10). Solomon asks Yahweh for a most special gift: 'Give your servant a listening heart so as to be able to discern' (1 Kings 3:9). The psalmist asks us to 'spend your night in quiet meditation' (Ps. 4:4); 'I will listen to what God the Lord will say.' (Ps. 85:8). 'Hear, O Israel: the Lord our God, the Lord is one' (Deut. 6:4). 'Listen to me, my people; hear me, my nation' (Isa. 50:4). 'Listen, listen. Pay attention, come to me; listen and you shall live' (Isa. 55:2–3).

In the New Testament we also find frequent commands to listen. 'This is my son, the beloved … Listen to him' (Mark 9:7). 'Listen to me, all of you, and understand' (Mark 7:14). 'When he said this, he called out, Those who have ears, let them hear' (Luke 8:8). 'Those along the path are the ones who hear' (Luke 8:12). 'Mary sat down at the Lord's feet and listened to him speaking' (Luke 10:39). 'My sheep listen to my voice; I know them and they follow me' (John 10:27). 'Today if you will hear his voice do not harden your hearts' (Heb. 3:7). 'Here I am! I stand at the door and knock. If any one hears my voice and opens the door, I will come in and eat with them and they with me' (Rev. 3:8). 'Let anyone who listens answer' (Rev. 13:9).

Soul Friend

We have already explored the term 'soul friend'. Another of its uses is as the Celtic name for a spiritual director, and this is the term I prefer. I sense we are not meant to be 'directors' as such, because even in their separateness the soul friend and the seeker are on a journey together. There are several basic needs on this journey: the ability to arrive at self-intimacy; the willingness to recognise and accept that each person is unique, that they come from differing backgrounds and expectations, have differing journeys and histories, and that these needs must be acknowledged and honoured; the readiness and the capacity to hear through the process of listening. Throughout this book I have used the word 'seeker' rather than 'speaker', in the belief that each person who needs a listener is seeking – searching for a way forward through growth that has been self-initiated with the courage of hope. For me the ideal listener, the one who really hears, is the soul friend who has a deepening respect for the seeker.

I suggest that the soul friend is the humanised ear of God, Jesus and the seeker. She is primarily concerned with being fully receptive to the seeker's situation, as together they discern the obstacles that may be blocking the seeker's journey towards wholeness. It is the soul friend's responsibility to be present, to encourage, and to prepare a breakthrough in the evolving life of the seeker, without any desire to tell him what to do. Only then, very occasionally, might she offer advice. Our task is to listen on the basis that the seeker has the solutions within himself, waiting to be acknowledged and thereby released. This will not necessarily occur in early meetings; patience with ourselves as listeners will ease the anxieties of the seeker, who may be guided more by silence than words; these may get in the way, as we wait together within the sacred space of sharing.

How, as a soul friend, do we prepare for 'being there' with the seeker? Well, silence and meditation are the foundations, when I ask God 'to give your servant a listening heart so as to be able to discern' (1 Kings 3:9). I may only take on this work to the extent that I am unafraid of being stripped of illusions, attachments, defences, egocentricity and false humility. It further means I am willing and hopefully prepared and open to the silences of solitude, that I might all the more become a channel of the transforming work of God, open to whatever direction the Holy Spirit may reveal.

I dare not offer myself, nor can I fully accept the responsibility of my call as a soul friend, unless I am prepared to love myself as I would love my neighbour, and even more so those with whom I would normally be uncomfortable. This means I must be prepared, to the best of my differing abilities, nurtured by the wound of my vulnerability, to carry out the basic commandment of Jesus: 'This is my commandment; love one another as I have loved you' (John 15:12). How do I continue to love others? 'As the Father has loved me, so have I loved you' (John 15:19). 'Because he loved first' (1 John 4:12, 19). Knowing that 'Love forgives all, trusts all, hopes all and endures all.'

How am I to love with the empathy of patience? 'Love is patient, loves tries to endure whatever happens' (1 Cor. 13:4, 7). I am called to love with the truth of love. 'Love rejoices in the truth' (1 Cor. 13:6). How do I love with the love of gentleness? 'Love is gentle, love does not delight in evil' (1 Cor. 13:5). How am I to love with humility? 'Love does not boast. It is not proud' (1 Cor. 13:4). How am I to love with love? 'Faith, hope and love, and the greatest of these is love' (1 Cor. 13:13).

Clearly the soul friend is a lover nurtured by a love that in turn nurtures the truth of our innate goodness, the courage to move forward in love one to the other. 'Bring awareness to the many subtle sounds of nature – the rustling of leaves in the wind, rain-drops falling, the humming of an insect, the first bird-song at dawn. Give yourself completely to the art of listening. Beyond the sounds there is something greater: a sacredness that cannot be understood through thought' (Tolle, *Stillness Speaks*, p. 79).

The soul friend is a listener who is unafraid of silence and is able to cope with the tensions. It will be a silence that radiates to the seeker that we matter to each other. Silence adds a different dimension to 'being there', in whatever space and time is needed by the seeker, to hear not only what the listener may have said but more importantly what is being stirred within seeker and listener alike. The spiritual director as soul friend rarely teaches in the ordinary sense. Rather she serves first as a listener who takes time to hear, eliciting acceptance and truthfulness. Homes comments, 'It is the province of knowledge to speak and it is the privilege of wisdom to listen.'

The *Rule For a New Brother* (or New Sister) spells this out quite well for us:

> Obedience also
> demands of you
> that you listen to the other person
> not only to what he is saying
> but to what he is.
> Then you will begin to live in such a way
> That you neither crush nor dominate
> Nor entangle your brother
> But help him to be himself.
> And lead him to freedom.
>
> (Anonymous, *Rule for a New Brother*, p. 118)

Paul Tournier, a famous Swiss doctor, was in general practice: he thought he knew all about patients until suddenly they began to talk to him on a deeper level. He once said, 'the level on which our patients are prepared to talk is dependent *on the level of our own availability*' (italics mine). We can only hear through listening according to the time we offer the seeker.

There is little doubt in my mind that how we care for ourselves will be how we care for others, be they seekers, members of our own family or extended family, friends or colleagues, or – perhaps of equal importance – those we have difficulty associating with ourselves. This caring is nurtured through our ability to love not only our neighbour as ourselves, but also those we may have difficulty understanding, or alongside whom we find it difficult to be. From my own experience, I found I was only able to begin to fulfil this basic law, and to be alongside others, when I began in earnest to love and accept my own self, with all my imperfections, wounds and growing inner strengths. This, coupled with the experience of being accepted and mattered, of being listened to and heard, enabled me to offer similar gifts to others. It further illustrated to me that all healing is circular. The basic truth is that there is no them and us; it is not 'there but for the grace of God go I', but rather 'there *with* the grace of love go I'.

At various times throughout my life the question has risen, 'Who am I?' Alongside it arises the equally important question, 'Whose am I?' It is from within this search that I have gradually become aware of the echo system, or rather the network of differing types of family within the community of humanity which cause me to ask: 'Do my family own me? Does society own me? Do the caring professions own me? Do those who come into the orbit of my concern own me? Does the Christian movement own me? Does Jesus the Christ own me? Does God own me? Do I own me?'

If we are to continue to live our lives fully then we must be constantly learning how to embrace the oneness of opposites, the oneness between our limits and our potential. We must be unafraid of hearing and honouring the truth of our limitations and our potential. The mutuality of hearing through listening can often release the deep cry of pain that is crucial if wounded seekers are to delve deeper into the meaning of their wounds, their vulnerabilities and how they can become resources for healing. I believe that seeded within every wound are the seeds of our healing. The more attentive our listening, the more the seeker will feel secure enough to reveal his or her needs for healing. As we continue to 'listen with intent' we shall have revealed to us the uniqueness lying deep within each person, the light of goodness and beauty of which the seeker has not been consciously aware.

12

Hearing into dying and death

Whom God loves, he loves to the end: and not only to their own end, to their death, but to his end; and his end is that he might love them still.

John Donne

So much of my ministry has involved me in being there with those who are dying and fearful of God's judgement. The only response I can make to this fear is that Christian spirituality is based on the gospel of love and forgiveness as mirrored in the life, ministry and death of Jesus.

Basic questions for the priest or pastor when first making contact with the dying or bereaved person are: How might we best recognise and accept where this person is within themselves spiritually? How might we meet their particular needs? Where the person is a Christian, then we may be able to connect with the local church community, but in today's society this is becoming more difficult. This may be because the Church does not speak to these people in their everyday lives, or because their experience of the Church has been unhelpful, possibly condemnatory or judgemental. Equally there are many who have never had any real connection with religion of any kind.

Stoll suggests that we can start by asking ourselves, 'What is the person's concept of God or duty? What is the person's source of hope or strength? What is the person's perceived relationship between their spiritual beliefs and their state of health? The aim is to identify areas of spiritual need and together plan the appropriate support.' All of us involved in this ministry must be extremely careful not to proselytise. This is a form of religious blackmail and nothing can be more damaging. Spiritual care, along with other forms of caring by differing persons and professions, should ensure that the needs of the pre-dying and the pre-bereaved will be met with the dignity of respect, through constant reassurance and understanding. This will be nurtured through the empathy of compassion and unassuming friendship, with access to the sacraments and rituals where appropriate, thereby offering the person an experience of being mattered, affirmed and loved.

It is our task to allow and enable the dying person to explore freely whatever doubts and fears he may have, without ridicule or rejection. In this way the pastor/priest opens the way for a spiritual ministry of being there for the dying person, as well as for the bereaved, within the differing stages of 'letting go'. This is the most human bridge for the dying person, living his or her life to the full in the now of this life and the next. There is a saying within the First Nation people of North America: 'It is good to live, it is good to die, it is good to live.' If we can take this on board ourselves, we may be able to offer some kind of assurance to the dying and the bereaved.

Caring for someone who is dying, however, is demanding spiritual work. It calls for the dignity of humility and the courage of faith in order to meet the various challenges that arise as the dying person begins to accept the limits of their life and begins to let go of the will to control. I believe it is very important for priests and others to realise that we are not responsible for this person's dying. However, we are responsible for insisting that she is able to die in the peace of her dignity, in the awareness that God does not know how to reject anyone.

Being with those who were dying as a result of the HIV/AIDS virus has taught me much, has deepened and enriched my own spiritual growth. I believe that a spirituality of life includes the spirituality of dying. In a sense they nurture each other, affirm our 'going forth' into the mystery of the greater life. It seems to me that life takes us out of life and that death takes us into life, the greater life that is beyond our comprehension.

Pastoral Care of the Dying
Pastoral care entails concern for a person's physical, mental and social pain, which may be the source of spiritual pain. For example, if I knew that I had hurt another and realised that I had never offered to apologise, that might be weighing on my mind;

or perhaps I had not forgiven someone who had hurt me and had held a grudge ever since; or I might feel guilty over something I had done and allowed someone else to take the blame. As a way of opening up to the healing of this pain I would discuss the situation with my soul friend, examining how best to make amends through prayer and action. Pain is often a subjective rather than an objective experience, but not always – objective pain calls for palliative treatment, and today pain, whatever its source, is increasingly recognised as a call for attention to be paid to that which is affecting normal body–mind functioning. It may also be a sign of healing and health.

It is our responsibility as pastoral listeners to encourage the seeker to be honest about their pain, be it physical or mental, i.e., depression, anxiety or fear. This enables us, with the seeker's permission, to be advocates towards initiating further assistance from other members of the care team. From my own experience of being in hospital I realised I should never say to the person in pain, 'I know how you feel.' This is impossible – I am not the other person, my history is not the same, even though I may have a similar background or outlook on life. All I can do in truth is to empathise through the pain I have experienced in my own life.

Throughout my life I have been present alongside many who were dying. They have shown me that they are spiritual by the way they live their dying with serenity, with a sense that all is well and all shall be well as they openly face the 'ultimate mystery'. They may have regarded religion as being an impersonal framework held together by a fabric of creeds and doctrines that have no meaning for them, but they are open to the ultimate mystery labelled 'God'. Although such people may not be 'religious' they have often revealed, in the way they faced death, something profoundly spiritual. I have often seen this as the person becomes more relaxed in his dying and alive *in the now* of the immediate situation. He is able to let go of the past with a sense of hope and a feeling of being embraced by a mystery.

People will quite often say, 'I'm not religious, but I am spiritual, I have lived a good life and I have not knowingly hurt another person or creature.' Or, 'I have my own beliefs about God.' The spiritual can be sensed in their request for a funeral or memorial service and for a priest to officiate – that the service may include the 23rd Psalm or the Lord's Prayer, the prayer attributed to St Francis or a Bible reading such as 1 Corinthians 13:1–13 or Revelations 21:1–7, a request for a hymn or a selection from Faure's *Requiem*. Some may desire a very simple service, others a Requiem mass; some may request a burial, others a cremation service; increasingly there is the request for burial or interment of the ashes in a woodland park rather than a cemetery.

Being alongside a young person who is dying, I have been able to recognise her innate spirituality, through such questions as 'Is there a God and if so where?' 'What is God?' 'Why does God allow suffering?' 'Is there a heaven?' 'Where is hell?' 'Will God accept me?' These questions suggest the young person is searching for a meaning, trying to find out whether she is acceptable to God. I believe such people are searching for a meaningful identity that will survive their death through a growing recognition and acceptance that they are related to the mystery of all creation, visible and invisible.

In the comfort of an unobtrusive presence the dying person will sometimes speak of her spiritual awareness, of a special presence in the room, even though initially that person may have said, 'I'm not religious, I don't go for God talk'. Perhaps my being there as myself with the empathy of compassion has enabled such people to discover their spirituality, to find that they have something to offer to the care team, to others and to God that gives meaning to their living into their dying.

The dying need to know they are loved by God, however God may be defined. All carers are called to be the human heart of God, reaching out to the heart and soul of the dying. This, hopefully, will enable the person to have a sense of being embraced by the love of God, through those who love and care for them.

My ministry has been personally enriched through the experience of caring for and with my partner, Richie, through his pre-dying grief and in his dying, in the silences we shared as he was preparing to flow into the greater mystery, taking with him his own unique gifts and mystery. I remember feeling, as we held each other, that we were both caught up in a mystery. Clearly life and death are a continuing part of one mystery. A reminder that life, death, and life nurtures our on-going and ever-changing journey into the greatest mystery that we call God.

It is important for pastors to quietly 'be there' with the dying person, offering them their attentiveness as they go through their 'dark night of the soul' with the light of hope, so that each person goes forth into the cloud of unknowing with an awareness of being embraced by love's infinity in the now of his or her dying.

The care that the pastor offers will be more relaxed if he recognises his own needs. I remember sharing a conference with Dr Sheila Cassidy at which we were both speakers. She made two powerful statements for those who would be carers in this field. I feel her statements are crucial to all who offer the presence of friendship, along with whatever care, sacraments or rituals are requested. She referred to the fact that Christian carers (along with carers of other faiths and none) should always try to take the paschal overview of suffering, that they should keep focus in the harsh reality of suffering and the mind-boggling truth of the resurrection – life after death. She also said that it was important for professional (and volunteer) carers to have the humility to recognise their own limitations, and to take *quality time out* for social relaxation, and silence, to avoid the real danger of burn-out.

I know from my own experience of not having taken this kind of self-care that this is sound advice, grounded in reality. I have no doubt that caring with and for the dying nurtures the spirituality of living within the circularity of our caring, that our lives are enriched through having the humility to allow the person labelled 'patient' to be caring of ourself.

Soul Quest

I remember William, a young man nearing the end of his life. As I sat alongside him, holding his hand during long periods of silence, William suddenly asked me, 'Father Bill, what is the soul and where does it go when I die?' I had to admit that I was not totally sure of what the soul is, that it was one of those questions that have constantly been debated throughout the history of humanity. I mentioned the fact that I believe the soul to be impregnated with the love of God and that it will return into what I call the soul of all creation. 'Have I got a soul?' William asked, and I replied, 'Your soul is yourself, being fully human.' William's response was, 'Well, Father Bill, I will know the answer before you. Please keep holding my hand. I'm going to go to sleep now. Everything is fine, thanks. I love you.'

William died during the same day. Soon afterwards we celebrated the service which he and his partner had designed for his friends and family.

13

Listening to the heartbeat of creation

It Wonders Me
It wonders me, it wonders me,
So beautiful a day can be –
So green the field,
So blue the sky,
So red and gold
The maple tree.

Somewhere a breeze begins to sing
Somewhere a bird is answering,
So wonderful sweet the melody,
It wonders me.

So green the field,
So blue the sky
So gold the tree,
It wonders me.

From Singers Musical Theatre Anthology, Vol. 2,
compiled and edited by Richard Walters, 2000

For me the Gospel of St John, with its songs of joy, pain and healing, is the 'Gospel of Love'. I love to hear it being read and
always, when hearing it, I have a sense of the tingling vibrations
of love: 'In the beginning was the Word, and the Word was with
God' (John 1:1). Yes, in the beginning was the Word Love. The
Word is God who, like Love, is a mysterious Word. John V.
Taylor writes:

If you can think of God at a time when nothing had yet been created, a time when there is no time, no space, nothing at all except limitless energy of love which we call God, what do you imagine God is thinking? What is he saying? He's thinking of love and the infinite purposes and promises of love. There is nothing else to be thought. And what is his response to those thoughts, those purposes and promises of love? What word do you feel he would say? 'Yes, O yes!' The 'yes' of delight and recognition, 'That's right', which an artist or a scientist shouts inwardly when he or she hits on a perfect solution. The 'Yes' of one who volunteers to carry out a superb plan when it has been made clear. Yes! So be it! Amen. (Taylor, *The Easter God*, p. 7)

The Divine plan is that we shall all 'Love your God with all your heart, with all your mind, with all your soul, and your neighbour as yourself.' Surely this plan is activated through having the courage of faith to love oneself, thereby liberating oneself for others, in the awareness that love is more than a word. It is the symbol activating the energies through the embracing of a fearless love.

In the Gospel of St John he is the one leaning against Jesus at the last supper; he is the image of the one who hears through listening to the heartbeat of God's love for all humanity. This same kind of listening is at the very heart of the Celtic church, having as it does a spirituality that is ever open towards all God's people and the fullness of his beloved creation. During the later part of the last century there developed an awareness of the fact that the Aboriginal, the Maori and the First Nation peoples of North America were and are very conscious of God, whatever their name for this mystery, enfleshed as it is in all creation. They looked, they saw, they heard, they touched, they smelt and knew a sense of God to be buried within themselves, in the all of life. They listened, they heard and they felt God to be in all things – in the growth of plants and trees, in the animals, the birds and the fishes of the sea. They heard God in the winds, the seas, the stars, the moon and sun, and in all animate and inanimate things. For them there was and is a growing sense of all life's energies emanating from within the mystery of God's mystery, constantly weaving the spiritual with the material, heaven with earth, the inner with the outer selves, male and female. 'He created them.'

'It wonders me', when I realise that all creation is called to be in constant communication between God and ourselves. Our prayers, along with our silences, our worship, all form part of the fabulous hymn of all creation, the oldest hymn that has been sung from the beginning of time. It is through this great hymn that we are humanised into our own becoming. Through this hymn of praise, and the spirituality of wonder, we are reminded that to become humanised is to become what our Creator desires us to be.

This is the main theme of the great Carmichael Collection, known as the *Gadelica* (which means simply 'the songs and poems of the Gaels'). These songs are rich in the celebration of the goodness of all creation. They are permeated with the belief that the grace of healing has been implanted within the goodness of creation. They view the life of God as being deep within creation as well as being distinct from it. They see a uniting distinction between God and the reverencing of creation. One of the great traits of Celtic spirituality is that of seeking God's presence in the whole of life, instead of exclusively within the Church and its traditions. The Celtic way for the Christian is followed through having time to practise listening for the eternal heartbeat of God, preparing us to go even deeper into the mystery, beyond life as we know and experience it.

Michael Morwood in *Praying a New Story* affirms the Church's early tradition in the wonder of all creation, visible and invisible:

> We believe that God is the Ground of everything that exists, that everything exists *in* God. Everything and everyone we see in this universe participates in God and gives God a way of coming to expression. We are products of God's creative presence in our universe for billions and billions of years. God's presence anywhere in the universe operates in and through what is there to be worked with. Earth is quite different from Venus, yet the same Presence is operative in each planet. So too with us. God works in and through what God has to work with: changing worldviews, different cultures, personalities, individual giftedness, institution-

alised religion, our developing knowledge about the universe and our planet, and human limitations. We are all connected *in* God and we give God wonderfully diverse ways of coming to visibility.

(Morwood, *Praying a New Story*, p. 47)

What he is saying is that all life is vibrant with the energies of God, as we are his

Listening to the Universe

I have learned throughout my journey as a listener to be alongside myself, as well as with others. In listening through hearing I am 'stilled' before the awesome presence of the seeker, in the awareness that we are both seekers.

To be sensitive to the soundless sounds of the universe in which we live, move and have our becoming is to be caught up in the wonder of nature, the experience of being a part of the living fabric of the wholeness of nature, rich in the diversity of her awesomeness. I remember, one early summer day, wandering with Richie, my partner, through the Trough of Bowland in Lancashire. Soon after we started our walk the sky clouded over; within seconds there was a downpour and we were soaked to the skin. We both said, 'Well, there's nothing for it but to strip.' And so we did, and the sensuousness of our bodies became alive as we were engulfed by the floodwaters of the thunderstorm. The next thing, we were rolling around in the 'glorious mud' and running through the forest from one puddle to the next until the sun came out – time to lie on the grass drying ourselves in the warmth, reading to each other from Aelred of Rievaulx's book, *Spiritual Friendship*. What a joyful experience of being caught up in the spirituality of life in all its sensuousness. We were enmeshed in the wonder of being 'oned' to the nature of God.

On another occasion, when I was staying with the Little Brothers of Jesus in the south of France, they suggested as part of my retreat that I might like to borrow a bicycle and ride through the cornfields. As I did so I passed through a tiny hamlet and on to a vast field of sunflowers, which reminded me of Van Gogh's marvellous paintings. I got off my bike and lay down among them, bathed in the glorious sun in its canopy of blue. Lying in the field, I felt I was being moved into a deeper sense of the oneness of all creation, a link between the mystery of heaven and earth.

Twenty years later I was visiting my family in Vancouver, having spent a wonderful week travelling around the Rockies of British Columbia. The rising and the setting of the sun, the awakening of the birds in the morning, were sheer bliss. One day I decided to visit Sandi, my grandniece, in West Vancouver. To get there, I decided to walk around Stanley Park and over Lion's Gate Bridge, which crosses over to West Vancouver. The total journey was about two hours, and by the time I reached the Park Royal shopping centre of West Vancouver my feet were so sore that I rang my niece to pick me up. Having arrived at her home, I sat in the lounge looking out to sea, my feet soon in a bowl of soothing water, while Sandi placed in my arms her latest baby, just one month old. As I gazed at wee Milan I felt aware that I was holding a very delicate miracle, and a wonderful glow flowed through me as we both fell asleep in each other's presence – indeed, it was the spiritual experience of a wonderful link between four generations.

Another wonder for me was seeing a red cell of my own blood under a very powerful microscope. I felt I was looking into the dark night of the sky, filled with shooting stars of many mineral colours. To see this was an awesome sight, if you like a 'spiritual sight' of the mystery of 'as above, so below; as within, so without' – a sign of the connectedness of creation's ongoing co-creativity.

These four experiences moved me with the wonders and voices of nature. I believe we are failing to listen 'with intent' to the differing sounds and pictures that make up the great symphony of creation as the greatest composers, poets and writers have done throughout the centuries. Sadly we are allowing ourselves to create the disasters that will eventually destroy that which offers us so much comfort and joy, the nurturing of our spiritualities; through our ever-increasing activity of pollution and exploitation – of each other, and especially of the poor, as well as the rivers, lakes and oceans; through the denuding of the world's forests for monetary profit; and not forgetting the many wars going on throughout the world. By so doing we are seriously wounding the planet that was meant to be a home for all peoples and all living creatures. Forgetting, as Julian of Norwich reminds us, that we are all 'oned to each other and to God'.

No wonder young people today say, 'Why bother? No one really cares about our future, or they would be doing something to encourage us that we have a future worth living for.' I believe that the great depression that so many young people feel had its birth in the bombing of Hiroshima and Nagasaki, where the mass slaughter of children, women, the infirm and the elderly was brought about by the dropping of two bombs. No longer were wars to be fought man to man – a tragedy for all human-ity unless we learn to listen and hear each other, putting aside our hidden agendas.

I believe that the following words, written by Helen Keller in 1933, are still equally relevant today. She urges us:

> Use your eyes as if tomorrow you would be stricken blind … hear the music of voices, the song of the bird, the mighty strains of the orchestra, as if you would be stricken deaf tomorrow. Touch each object as if tomorrow your tactile sense would fail. Smell the perfume of the flowers, taste with relish each morsel, as if tomorrow you could never smell or taste again. Make the most of your senses: glory in all the facets of pleasure and beauty, which the world reveals to you.
>
> (Breathnach, *Romancing the Ordinary*, p. 1)

We are all called to be co-artists, as well as co-creators with God, nurtured through our evolving spiritualities and the glory of wonder.

Psalm 148 calls the whole universe to praise the creator. The psalmist delights in calling the different parts of creation – the angels; the heavenly bodies, sun, moon and stars; the earth, the sea, the weather, all plants and animals; and all human beings. All are part of the great worshipping community of humanity. But the psalm ends with a reminder of his goodness to Israel, the people he brought close to himself, which is now the mission of the Christian community, alongside other faith communities.

Children want to touch everything, to smell flowers, taste the leaves, dangle their feet in the water, pick apart the scraps, carry home the bones. Sometimes I am impatient about their desire for direct contact. 'Have respect' I want to say but in the end I hold my tongue, knowing they pay their respects by making sensual contact with the world. 'The opposite of love', a friend reminds me, 'is not hatred, but indifference.'

(Paul Gruchow, quoted in Gardner (ed.),
The Sacred Earth, p. 36)

14
Afterword

Love is the spiritual drama on which the world depends
Howard Cooper

The main theme of *The Creativity of Listening*, illustrated along the way with stories and autobiographical notes, has been the activity of hearing through listening: to myself, with the aid of others; to the other person, in a one to one situation; and to the community, local, national and international.

In a deep sense we are all born with the potential to be either co-creative or co-destructive of each other. Hearing enlists our co-creativeness, while non-hearing enlists our co-destructiveness. There is no doubt that we who are both speaker and listener are also ourselves seekers. I have illustrated through my own experience and those of others the awareness that the wounds of our imperfections have seeded within them our potential for healing and growth. We are all empowered through in-depth communication, including that of silence, the very fabric of any relationship.

Throughout the book I have outlined and drawn upon several differing ways that have spoken to me, creative listening, pastoral listening and labyrinth walking among them, as effective aids towards healing. I have selected words that I consider vital in all this work: dignity and mattering, along with empathy and compassion. They are nurtured through our awareness of the other person's innate dignity and need to be mattered, and of our own.

New ways of thinking and of releasing the faith have been opened up for me by William Countryman, a theologian with a new vision of the priesthood of all believers, and Wayne Teasdale, a monk of the inner city. They speak to me through their differing visions. They echo my own thoughts in their co-creative, co-spiritual evolution of the Christ's faith in us, with new and liberating ways of ministry. Countryman writes of the priesthood of all believers – one priesthood with two dimensions, reminding us all that we are equalled through the basic rite of baptism. Wayne Teasdale, like many others, is aware that each faith in its uniqueness contains differing insights of the same mystery of the natural interfaithness of God and Christ towards all their 'Rainbow Peoples' who are the Sons and Daughters of God, Sisters and Brothers of Christ. Clearly all are seeded with the differing aspects of spirituality and many more are becoming aware of the interspiritual and intermystical that bonds all people together, thereby nurturing a spiritual, revelational activity for all humanity, all creatures, our earth, the cosmos, all embraced within the acceptance of God the Father, Mary the Mother, Jesus the Christ our Brother, embracing us with the Holy Spirit of love.

Along with thousands, perhaps millions of others, I sense the gradual evolution of a new spiritual movement which is being recognised as we move through the time of crisis affecting everyone and every creature in the world. It is a spirituality that is evolving within the chaos of our times. Edward Lorenz reminds us that chaos theory should enable those of all faiths and of none to define a new attitude towards each other, all nature, mother earth, and the whole cosmos. We will move through the present crisis by a healthy, healing management presented by chaos and the symphonic changes brought about through listening and hearing.

We are assisted in this great work if we realise that change is the eternal flow that enables all forms of life and living to evolve. Hopefully this will coincide with our personal and corporate evolution of who we are becoming and what we leave for those who will inherit not only the best, but also the worst. We do so by taking risks in order to be alongside both others and ourselves, knowing that for life to be fully lived co-creatively demands changes within and around ourselves.

> *Listening may begin as a one-way operation, but it can never be that for long. In the silence of our listening we are communicating implicitly with the other person in a language other than words, and thus revealing to him what we are. And the time will*

come when our self-revelation will become verbally explicit. Our relationship will cease to be apparently one way, as if we were the Good Samaritan and the other the wounded victim, because we shall realise that in order to be healed the other needs to see our own ugly wounds, to encounter us in our sickness as well as in our health, just as we are beginning to encounter him in his health as well as in his sickness. We shall discover that both the sickness and the health are things we have in common, so that both can become a bond between us. And as in this way we share what we are with each other we shall discover that it is in each other that we live.

H. A. Williams, *The Joy of God*, p. 70

A Prayer for Gifts

We pray for gifts
awakening us to the
gifts of hearing-listening
emanating from the heart

We pray for gifts
awakening us to the
awesome wonder of
creation's evolving creativity

We pray for gifts
awakening us to the
wounds inflicted on
all peoples, creatures
and Mother Earth.

We pray for gifts
awakening us to
the innate dignity,
uniqueness of all
persons, all creatures.

We pray for gifts
awakening us to the mystery of
gender orientation,
differing sexualities and
their co-creative potential.

We pray for gifts
awakening us to
the violence we
inflict on each other,
upon differing ministries.

We pray for gifts
awakening us to
the wounds of
addiction – be they
physical, mental, social,
emotional and/or spiritual.

We pray for gifts
awakening us to
the misuse of
power by fanatical
religious and political
fundamentalism.

We pray for gifts
awakening us to
the violence of
armaments nurtured
by the powers
of greed and fear.

We pray for gifts
awakening us to
accepting, we all
emerge into this
world through the
mystery of birth,
to live fully the
mystery of our lives
as we journey
forward into the
greater mystery embracing
all creation with
love's compassion
justice and hope.

BK
November 2004

Bibliography

The Jerusalem Bible, Darton Longman & Todd, 1967

Holy Bible: New International Version, Hodder & Stoughton, 1996

Anonymous, *The Rule for a New Brother*, Darton Longman & Todd, 1986

Artress, Lauren, *Walking A Sacred Path: Rediscovering the Labyrinth as a Spiritual Tool*, Riverhead Books, 1996

Barrett, Mark OSB, *Crossing: Reclaiming The Landscape of Our Lives*, Darton Longman & Todd, 2001

Berendt, Joachim-Ernst, *The Third Ear: On Listening to the World*, Element Books, 1988

Bianchi, Enzo, *Words of Spirituality: Towards a Lexicon of the Inner Life*, SPCK, 2002

Bloom, Anthony, *Meditations on a Theme*, Continuum, 2003

Brandon, David, *Zen in The Art of Helping*, Penguin, 1988

   Tao of Survival: Spirituality in Social Care and Counselling, Venture Press, 2000

Boyle, Jimmy, *A Sense of Freedom*, Pan, 1977

Breathnach, Sarah Ban, *Romancing The Ordinary*, Simon & Schuster, 2003

Cassidy, Sheila, *Sharing The Darkness: The Spirituality of Caring*, Darton Longman & Todd, 2000

Chardin, Teilhard de, Pierre, *Le Milieu Divin*, Collins, 1960.

Cleary, Thomas (ed.), *The Essential Koran: The Heart of Islam*, HarperCollins, 1994

Cooper, Howard, *The Alphabet of Paradise: An A–Z of Spirituality for Everyday Life*, Darton Longman & Todd, 2002

Countryman, L. William, *Living On the Border of the Holy: Renewing the Priesthood of All*, Morehouse Publishing, 1999

Dass, Ram and Gorman, Paul, *How Can I Help?: Stories and Reflections On Service*, Alfred A. Knopf, 1992

Downey, Michael, *Altogether Gift: A Trinitarian Spirituality*, Dominican Publications, 2000

Doherty, Catherine de Hueck, *Poustinia: Christian Spirituality of the East for Western Man*, Ave Maria Press, 1975

Farmer, Dr. E. (ed.), *Exploring Dimensions of Spiritual Care*, Quay Books, 1996

Ferder, Fran, *Words Made Flesh: Scripture, Psychology and Human Communication*, Ave Maria Press, 2000

Ferder, Fran and Heagle, John, *Tender Fires: The Spiritual Promise of Sexuality*, Crossroad Publishing, 2002

Fisher, Maggie, *The Therapeutic Use of Labyrinths*, Sacred Space Publications, 2003

Fromm, Erich, *The Art of Listening*, Constable, 1994

Gardner, Jason (ed.), *The Sacred Earth: Writers on Nature and Spirit*, New World Library, 1998

Griffin, Emilie, *Doors Into Prayer*, Darton Longman & Todd, 2003

Griffin, Emilie (ed.), *Evelyn Underhill: Essential Writings*, Orbis, 2003

Hall, Thelma, *Too Deep For Words: Rediscovering Lectio Divina*, Paulist Press, 1988

Harrington, Donal, *Prayer: Reflection for Group Meetings*, Columba Press, 2004

Harvey, Andrew, *The Essential Mystics: The Soul's Journey into Truth*, HarperSanFrancisco, 1996

Housden, Roger, *Soul and Sensuality: Returning The Erotic To Everyday Life*, Rider, 1993

Howell, Michael and Ford, Peter, *The True History of The Elephant Man*, Penguin, 1981

Ind, Jo, *Memories of Bliss: God, Sex and Us*, SCM Press, 2003

Jackson, Carl, *The Gift To Listen: The Courage to Hear*, Augsburg Books, 2003

Kearney, Tim (ed.), *A Prophetic Cry: Stories of Spirituality and Healing Inspired by L'Arche*, Veritas, 2000

Keck, Robert L., *Sacred Eyes: An Invitation to View the Entire Human Journey and Your Own*, Green Books, 1998

 Sacred Quest: The Evolution and Future Of the Human Soul, Chrysalis Books, 2000

 Healing as a Sacred Path: A Story Of Personal, Medical and Spiritual Transformation, Chrysalis Books, 2002

Kornfield, Jack, *After the Ecstasy, the Laundry: How the Heart Grows Wise on the Spiritual Path*, Bantam, 2001

Kurtz, Ernest and Ketcham, Katherine, *The Spirituality of Imperfection: Storytelling and the Journey to Wholeness*, Bantam, 1997

Kirkpatrick, Bill, *Going Forth: A Practical and Spiritual Approach to Dying and Death*, Darton Longman & Todd, 1997

Kyle, William, *The Wholeness of Man*, Westminster Pastoral Foundation pamphlet, 1980

Laszlo, Ervin, *You Can Change the World: Action Handbook for the 21st Century*, Positive News Publishing, 2002

Laszlo, Ervin, Grof, Stanislav, Russell, Peter, (eds), *The Consciousness Revolution*, Elf Rock, 2003

Leech, Kenneth, *Spirituality and Pastoral Care*, Cowley Publications, 1989

Lonegren, Sig, *Labyrinths: Ancient Myths and Modern Uses*, Gothic Image, 2000

Matthew the Poor, *Orthodox Prayer Life: The Interior Way*, St Vladimir's Press, 2003

McMullen, Richie, *Tom's Comments: Counselling for the Speaker*, discussion paper, 1983

McNamara, William, *Earthly Mysticism: Contemplation and the Life of Passionate Presence*, Crossroad Publishing, 1983

 Mystical Passion, Paulist Press, 1977

Mann, Ivan, *A Double Thirst: Reaching Beyond Suffering*, Darton Longman & Todd, 2001

Mayeroff, Milton, *On Caring*, Harper & Row, 1991

Mayne, Michael, *Pray, Love, Remember*, Darton Longman & Todd, 2000

Moore, Thomas, *Care Of The Soul*, new edn, Piatkus, 2004

Moran, Francis M., *Listening: A Pastoral Style*, E. J. Dwyer, 1997

Morwood, Michael, *Praying a New Story*, Orbis, 2004

Mother Mary Clare SLG, *Encountering the Depths*, Darton Longman & Todd, 1981

Newman, John Henry, *Prayers, Meditations and Devotion*, Ignatius Press, 1903

Nichol, Donald, *Holiness*, new edn, Darton Longman & Todd, 2004

Nouwen, Henri J. M., *The Wounded Healer: Ministry in Contemporary Society*, Darton, Longman & Todd, 1994
  Clowning in Rome, Darton, Longman & Todd, 2001
  Outside of Solitude: Three Meditations on the Christian Life, Ave Maria Press, 2003
  The Way of the Heart, Darton Longman & Todd, 2003
Nouwen, Henri, McNeill, Donald P., Morrison, Douglas A., *Compassion*, Darton Longman & Todd, 1990
O'Donoghue, Noel Dermot, *Heaven In Ordinarie: Prayer as Transcendence*, T. & T. Clark, 1996
O'Donohue, John, *Anam Cara: Spiritual Wisdom from the Celtic World*, new edn, Bantam Press, 1999
  Divine Beauty: The Invisible Embrace, Transworld, 2003
O'Hanlon, Gerry SJ, *Windows on Social Spirituality*, Columba Press, 2003.
Oppenheimer, Helen, *Making Good*, SCM Press, 2001
  'Mattering', *Studies in Christian Ethics* Vol. 8, No. 1, 1995
Owings, Timothy L., *Hearing God in a Noisy World: Prayer as Listening*, Peake Road, 1998.
Palmer, Parker J., *Let Your Life Speak: Listening For the Voice of Vocation*, Jossey-Bass, 2000
Pinney, Rachel, *Creative Listening*, A–Z Printers, 1983
Pembroke, Neil, *The Art of Listening: Dialogue, Shame and Pastoral Care*, T. & T. Clark/Handsel Press, 2002
Price, Peter B., *Playing the Blue Note: Journeying into Hope*, Darton Longman & Todd, 2002
Pym, Jim, *Listening to the Light: How to Bring Quaker Simplicity and Integrity into Our Lives*, Rider, 1999
  You Don't Have to Sit On the Floor: Bringing the Insights and Tools of Buddhism into Everyday Life, Rider, 2001
Reik, Theodor, *Listening with the Third Ear: The Inner Experience of a Psychoanalyst*, Farrar, Straus & Giroux, 1983
Rogers, Murray and Barton, David, *Abhishiktananda: A Memoir of Dom Henri Le Saux*, SLG Press, 2001
Rolheiser, Roland, *The Holy Longing: A Search for a Christian Spirituality*, Doubleday, 1999
Rowan, John, 'Listening as a Four Level Activity', *British Journal of Psychotherapy* Vol. 1 (4), 1985
Ryrie, Alexander, *Wonderful Exchange: An Exploration of Silent Prayer*, Canterbury Press, 2003
Sacks, Jonathan, *Dignity of Difference: How to Avoid the Clash of Civilisations*, new edn, Continuum, 2003
Sands, Helen Raphael, *Labyrinth: Pathway to Meditation and Healing*, Gaia Books, 2000
Schaper, Donna and Camp, Carole Ann, *Labyrinths From the Outside In: Walking to Spiritual Insight*, Skylight Paths Publishing, 2000
Searle, Joan, *The Importance of Listening*, Guild of Health, 1989
Seddon, Phillip, *The Whole Christ: The Spirituality of Ministry*, SLG Press, 1996
Sellner, Edward C., *Mentoring: The Ministry of Spiritual Kinship*, Cowley Publications, 2002

Shafir, Rebecca Z., *The Zen of Listening: Mindful Communications in the Age of Distraction*, Quest Books, 2003

Shaw, Gilbert, *The Holy Spirit*, card, SLG Press, 1968

Sheldrake, Rupert and Fox, Matthew, *Natural Grace: A Dialogue on Science & Spirituality*, Bloomsbury, 1999

Simpson, Ray, *Soul Friendship: Celtic Insights Into Spiritual Mentoring*, Hodder & Stoughton, 1999

Snidle, Heather and Yoeman, Paul, *Christ in AIDS: An Educational Pastoral Approach to HIV/AIDS*, Cardiff Academic Press, 1997

Steere, Douglas, *Where Words Come From*, London, Friends Home Service, 1985
   Gleanings: A Random Harvest, Upper Room Books, 1996

Stou, R., 'Guidelines for Spiritual Assessment', *American Journal of Nursing*, Sept. 1979

Swinton, John, *A Space To Listen*, Mental Health Foundation, 2001

Taylor, John V., *The Easter God, The Easter People*, Continuum, 2003

Teasdale, Wayne, *The Mystic Heart: Discovering a Universal Spirituality in the World's Religions*, New World Library, 1999
   A Monk in the World: Cultivating A Spiritual Life, New World Library, 2002

Thibodeaux, Mark, *Armchair Mystic*, St Anthony Press, 2001

Tolle, Eckhart, *The Power of Now*, Hodder & Stoughton, 2001
   Stillness Speaks, Hodder & Stoughton, 2003

Tomatis, Aelfred A. *The Conscious Ear: My Life of Transformation through Listening*, Station Hill Press, 1992

Tschudin, Verena, *Hearing Ourselves*, Marshall Pickering, 1989

Underhill, Evelyn, *The Spiritual Life: Great Spiritual Truths for Everyday Life*, One World Publications, 1999

Weil, Simone, *Waiting on God*, Routledge & Kegan Paul, 1951

Yalom, Irwin D., *The Gift of Therapy: Reflections on Being a Therapist*, Piatkus, 2002

Young, Andrew, *A Way Out of No Way: The Spiritual Memoirs of Andrew Young*, Thomas Nelson, 1996

Index